Hoover Institution Publications 138

Political Corruption: The Ghana Case

POLITICAL CORRUPTION
The Ghana Case

Victor T. Le Vine

Hoover Institution Press
Stanford University
Stanford, California

Library of Congress Cataloging in Publication Data

Le Vine, Victor T
    Political corruption; the Ghana case.

    (Hoover Institution publications, 138)
    Bibliography: p.
    1. Corruption (in politics)--Ghana. 2. Ghana--Politics and government. I. Title. II. Series: Stanford University. Hoover Institution on War, Revolution, and Peace. Publications, 138.
JQ3029.5.C6L4   320.9'667'05   74-13629
ISBN 0-8179-1381-5

Hoover Institution Publications 138
International Standard Book Number 0-8179-1381-5
Library of Congress Catalog Card Number 74-13629
© 1975 by the Board of Trustees of the
    Leland Stanford Junior University
All rights reserved
Printed in the United States of America

The sweetness of the pudding is in the eating thereof!
Attributed to Krobo Edusei, in reference to the perquisites of power.

Socialism is a system in which if you have a lot of money you can still keep it.
Krobo Edusei

In this country it was socialism for the poor and capitalism for the rich.
A Ghanaian citizen, after the 1966 coup.

Half-starved people are being daily admonished to tighten their belts, when members of the new Ghanaian aristocracy and their hangers-on, who tell them to do this, are fast developing pot bellies and paunches and their wives and sweethearts double chins in direct proportion to the rate at which people tighten their belts.
Victor Owusu, member of the parliamentary opposition until 1966, later Foreign Minister in the Busia government. Statement made in 1961.

Contents

Acknowledgments

This study deals with a subject that may arouse misgivings among some well-intentioned friends of Africa, and indeed the very fact that I have discussed it might leave me open to charges of bias or ethnocentricity. Therefore I feel I must go beyond the usual "you're not to blame" statements and grant the friends, advisers, and collaborators who aided me in this endeavor unconditional absolution. This does not relieve them of my gratitude, however: they have that in abundance.

My first and largest debt is to those friends and colleagues at the University of Ghana—both Ghanaian and non-Ghanaian—who urged me to undertake this study; without their unfailing support and advice what follows could not have been written. A number of other professional colleagues provided valuable counsel and insights, and some were kind enough to show me unpublished materials on Ghana and political corruption: Herbert Werlin, Beverley Pooley, Richard Rathbone, Richard Crook, David Apter, and John Esseks. Peter Duignan and Lewis Gann of the Hoover Institution read the manuscript, and I am grateful for their criticisms and comments as well as for their hospitality and many kindnesses during my summer at Palo Alto. I have also profited from the valuable advice of several colleagues at Washington University; including James Davis, John Kautsky, and Kenneth Shepsle. I owe more than I can properly acknowledge to my colleague Arnold J. Heidenheimer, also at Washington University, who read the manuscript and whose seminal contributions to the study of political corruption find frequent mention in these pages. Finally, I wish to thank the Hoover Institution for the stipend and access to research materials it afforded in the summer of 1972, and for the support that permitted the first draft of this study to be completed in the peace and quiet of the Hoover Tower at Stanford University.

A Note on Ghanaian Currency

Monetary values cited in chapters 2–6 are reported in the currency in use at the time. Until independence (1957) the British pound (£), worth roughly $2.80, was in use. After independence until July 1965, the Ghanaian pound (G £), at par with the British pound, was the currency. (The Commissions of Inquiry appointed after the 1966 coup often reported sums in either or both British and Ghanaian pounds, since the two were equal in value. Our citations follow that usage.) From July 1965 until February 1967 Ghana's currency was the Cedi (₵), worth $1.16. From February 1967 to July 1967 the New Cedi (N₵) was worth $1.40. In July 1967 Ghana devalued her currency, and until December 1971 the New Cedi was worth $.98. In December 1971, the New Cedi was devalued by 44 percent, but soon after the February 1972 military coup it was revalued once again. The New Cedi is presently worth about $.65.

Introduction

The subject of this study is political corruption in Ghana. I define political corruption as the unscheduled, unsanctioned use of public political resources and/or goods for private, that is, non-public, ends. A detailed elaboration of this definition is contained in chapter 1.

The Study: Background and Scope

Ghana was chosen as the focus of the study because circumstances took the author there at a time when the country was uniquely and intensely preoccupied with the problem of corruption in its midst.[1] It may be that a good part of that preoccupation resulted from the revelations of the more than forty Commissions of Inquiry[2] that were appointed during the 1966–69 period by the National Liberation Council (NLC) government in an attempt to discredit the preceding regime—the regime headed by Kwame Nkrumah from 1951 to 1966. Indeed, since so massive a series of revelations about any wrongdoing in government could not fail to excite widespread public interest and introspection, it is perhaps more significant that of all the denigrative themes the NLC might have chosen, it chose *corruption* as the theme most likely to be widely understood and to have the greatest public impact. Whatever the reasons for this preoccupation, it remained undiminished six years after the collapse of the Nkrumah regime: the country's leading newspapers and journals were still filled with reports of corruption and discussions of causes, effects, and cures; the Busia government, which succeeded the NLC, appointed its own special commission to look into the problem in its broad aspects; and no week passed in which Ghanaian officials at all levels of government, religious leaders and heads of other organizations, and various publicists and scholars failed to discuss the matter of corruption publicly and inveigh, caution, or preach against its evils. Thus, whereas normally it is exceedingly difficult to find any documentation on political corruption anywhere, Ghana, in some of its public documents and particularly in the reports of its committees and Commissions of Inquiry, provided an abundance of detailed materials on a wide range of corrupt practices and behaviors. How reliable were these sources? In my judgment, the Commissions on the whole did their work honestly and judiciously, and the reports they produced were unusual in their adherence to the facts and their fairness to those under investigation. (This issue is also discussed on p. 135, n. 47.) Ghana became the focus of this study, then, not because it or Ghanaians are particularly prone to political corruption (for political corruption is endemic to virtually every political system) or because Ghanaian political corruption is for any other reason particularly noteworthy, but because I happened to be there when I was, and reliable data were available to permit a detailed inspection of the process in its manifold aspects. While the hard data relate to Ghana, the analytic model developed in these pages may well have wider applications.

This study does not deal with the moral aspects of corrupt behavior, although much of the material on which it is based is distinctly moralizing in tone. Certainly the NLC Commissions of Inquiry did not stint at passing judgment on the activities of groups and persons involved in the Nkrumah regime. Certainly too, apologists for the Nkrumah regime, as well as its more sober analysts, have commented extensively on the moral implications of public corruption in Ghana during that period; to find such comments in discussions ranging from passionate defense to dispassionate analysis, one need only consult the published work of Nkrumah himself, or that of Geoffrey Bing (Nkrumah's former Attorney General) or Sam Ikoku (a Nigerian who became an important Party spokesman), and the relevant studies and monographs by Fitch and Oppenheim, David Apter, Scott Thompson, Roger Genoud, Henry Bretton, and T. Peter Omari.[3] And certainly at least some of those involved in corrupt practices in Ghana (see Chapter 3) passed explicit or implicit judgment on their own behavior as well as that of their peers. Rather, I am concerned to argue that politically corrupt behavior has visible consequences for a political system apart from all questions of whether such behavior is in itself good or bad. With this emphasis, arguments about the uses of corruption (as advanced by Nathaniel Leff, for example) and assessments of its costs and benefits (*vide* Joseph Nye) become part of the more general consideration of consequences.[4] In any event, an empirical examination of consequences is certain to contribute more to an understanding of political corruption than the roundest condemnation.

Because of its emphasis on political, i.e., public, corruption, this study does not consider corruption in the private sector of the economy except insofar as it affected the more widespread corruption in the public arena. Furthermore, it deals only marginally with the relationship between Ghanaian political corruption and the structures and institutions of the once-dominant Convention Peoples Party (CPP). CPP leaders and members are discussed as they were involved in corruption, but we avoid the argument advanced by James C. Scott in his excellent comparative study of political corruption that the CPP exemplified a "machine-politics" regime.[5] There are some very real questions about the solidity of the CPP's supportive base and the effectiveness of its operations, and in fact there is some doubt that the CPP was ever a mass political party. There is reason to believe that its "machine" appearance was more façade than reality. Undeniably, the party looked like a machine while Nkrumah was in power, particularly in the major towns of the south; yet below the District Commissioner level it had little substance and apparently operated mainly to turn out people for rallies and official visits and to assist in raising—or extorting—money for the party coffers. In any case, no one has yet explained why this "machine" disappeared so rapidly all over the country in February 1966, leaving behind only a froth of disgruntled bureaucrats and trapped politicians, when by all accounts it had been not only solidly entrenched but adept at grass-roots mobilization.

Finally, it is possible that some may see this study as a post mortem on the government of Dr. K. A. Busia, which was overthrown on January 14, 1972, by a military coup. This is certainly not my intention, nor is it intended that the reader conclude that political corruption was the prime cause of Dr. Busia's downfall although, as I shall argue, it may have been a contributory factor. One of the first acts of the new government of Col. Ignatius K. Acheampong in 1972 was to launch several probes into the assets and activities of his predecessors, the most important being the Commission headed by Justice Taylor. Thus far, the revelations of these probes have hardly been as sensational as those of the NLC Commissions. If it can be argued that this is so because the Ghanaian public is no longer shocked by revelations of wrongdoing on the part of its leaders and high officials, it is also probable that any pillage of the public treasury that took place under the Busia regime simply did not reach the levels attained during 1962–65.

Ghana: A Brief Political History

A full understanding of the analysis developed in the pages that follow requires some awareness of the political history of Ghana between the end of the Second World War and 1973. Many readers will be unfamiliar with that background, and others may find it useful to have it recalled. Hence, a broad review of the salient aspects of Ghanaian political history is included here to highlight key points of reference in this study and to place those events in chronological perspective. More detailed treatment of the subject is available in a number of authoritative works cited later in this Introduction.

Ghana is the name given the British colony formerly known as the Gold Coast when it attained independence in 1957. The present name evokes the half-mythical glories of the ancient sub-Saharan kingdom of Ghana, which flourished in the western Sudan between the eighth and tenth centuries A.D.; the name was revived at the time of independence as a symbol of both the pride of self-rule and the African authenticity of the new state. Ghana's existence as a political entity, however, derives more from territorial divisions made during the colonial period than from the several local African kingdoms that were established in the area before the advent of complete European domination.

Between the fifteenth and nineteenth centuries A.D., the Portuguese, English, Danes, Swedes, French, Dutch, and Germans established trading enclaves and forts along the Ghana coast. By the beginning of the nineteenth century, Britain had gained control of most of the coastal and coastward areas. In the process, it had begun to come into contact with the traditional Ashanti state, which had dominated the central and south-central parts of the territory since the beginning of the eighteenth century. The Ashanti, who had long hoped to extend their sway to the sea, now found the British barring their way. In 1874 Kumasi, the stronghold of Ashanti power was taken by a British force, and a southern Colony was established. In 1901, having finally overcome the last of the Ashanti resistance, as well as African resistance in the north, the British turned the Northern territories into a Protectorate; the Protectorate was added to the Southern Colony, and the British conquest of the Gold Coast was complete.

In 1922 Britain was given supervision over a part of the former German Togoland protectorate through a League of Nations mandate. The mandated territory, which lay to the east of the Colony and Protectorate, was administered as an integral part of the Gold Coast. It became a United Nations trusteeship in 1946, and following a UN-sponsored plebiscite in 1956, became part of the soon-to-be independent Gold Coast. The northern portion of the Togo territory contained an ethnically heterogeneous population; the southern part, however, was dominated by Ewe-speaking peoples who, before the plebiscite, had agitated for the creation of an autonomous Ewe state in which Ewes living in neighboring French Togo would be reunited with those under British administration. Subsequently, the Ewe, one of Ghana's most vigorous peoples, were alternately wooed and neglected by successive Ghanaian regimes; they continue to figure prominently in the politics of the country.

During the colonial period the British devolved a good deal of local authority to the traditional chiefs in an attempt to enlist their support. This policy, known as indirect rule, was markedly successful in the north, where African contacts with European influences were limited and traditional rulers retained considerable power. In the south, however, the policy had mixed results. Some of the coastal chiefs, notably the most influential ones among the Fanti and Ga, readily made peace with the British; the Ashanti chiefs, partly because of their long opposition to colonial rule and partly because of the strong Ashanti tradition of political cohesion, showed greater reservation. Moreover, the stronger Westernizing influences in the south tended to create challenge rather than acquiescence to British rule. Expanding economic opportunities, the impulse toward material improvement, and above all, sociopolitical ideas acquired in mission and government schools led many Africans to resent the inequities of the colonial system.

The Gold Coast proved a particularly fertile field for the growth of nationalist sentiment. A relatively benevolent administration, intensive missionary activity, effective official and voluntary agency schools, and prosperous coastal trade combined to produce a small but well-to-do African middle class composed of articulate teachers, ministers of the gospel, publicists, lawyers, and businessmen. These persons animated various groups striving for a greater African voice in the running of colonial affairs. Before the Second World War, a number of prominent Gold Coast men (some of whom served on the Colony's Legislative Council) emerged as leaders of nationalist groups. Among them were such figures as Joseph E. Casely-Hayford, Africanus Horton, Jr., John Mensah Sarbah, and Samuel R. B. At-toh-Ahuma.

At the end of the Second World War the British Governor, Sir Alan Burns, promulgated a new Constitution for the Gold Coast which for the first time gave political power to the eighteen elected African members on the 30-member Legislative Council. The end of the war also saw the return of thousands of Ghanaian veterans, who unfortunately found their country beset with shortages of consumer goods, inflation, black-market practices, and unemployment. These veterans formed a nucleus for gathering forces of discontent. Before long they were joined by farmers who resented government attempts to control the swollen-shoot disease infesting cocoa plantings (by cutting out the affected trees), and who moreover were growing increasingly disgruntled at the fact that the much-promised end-of-war economic prosperity was failing to materialize.

In August 1947, a nationalist party called the United Gold Coast Convention (UGCC) was formed. Its leader, Dr. Joseph Boakye Danquah, was an intellectual and lawyer whose past activities had been in the tradition of prewar Ghanaian nationalism. Danquah, however, went beyond the perspectives of the old Gold Coast elite in framing the new party and its goals. For the first time, he sought mass support for a program that included revision of the Burns constitution to provide for African ministers in the cabinet, and pushed for the earliest possible attainment of self-government. It was Danquah who harked back to the traditions of medieval Ghana to inspire a break with the colonial past and arouse ardor for the formation of the new state. It was also Danquah who in December 1947 invited Kwame Nkrumah to return home from his studies abroad and become executive secretary of the UGCC. Nkrumah had left Ghana in 1935 to study first at Lincoln University, then at the University of Pennsylvania, and finally, in London.

In the meantime, simmering discontent with the country's economic conditions had begun to boil over. Veterans and other groups instituted a boycott of imported goods that led at first to sporadic protests and ultimately, in February 1948, to widespread rioting in several major towns. The February trouble began in Accra, the Gold Coast capital, when a sizable protest march led by veterans deviated from its prescribed route and headed for the Governor's residence. Police halted the column, then opened fire, killing two of the marchers and wounding five; one of the dead was Sergeant C. F. Adjetey, the veterans' most respected leader. In the wake of the disturbances that followed, Ussher Prison in Accra was stormed and its inmates were released, and numerous European and Asian places of business in various towns were looted and destroyed. Before order was finally restored, some 29 people had been killed and 266 injured. The UGCC immediately seized on the official handling of the disturbances to launch renewed criticism of the government; so effective was its campaign that Danquah, Nkrumah, and several other UGCC leaders were arrested and deported to the Northern Territories.

As a result of the unrest, the British government sent out an investigative commission headed by Aiken Watson, a prominent British lawyer. The Watson Commission took note of the country's economic condition, roundly condemned a variety of corrupt practices that appeared to have exacerbated matters, and blamed the riots on the disturbed economy and on agitation by groups and persons it did not name. The Commission did find that Nkrumah sought to use "legitimate economic grievances" to stage a revolution with the aim of establishing a "union of West African Soviet Socialist Republics." It recommended, among other things, that the Burns Constitution be revised to give Africans a greater share in the government.

At the beginning of 1949 the Governor appointed an all-African committee chaired by Justice Henley Coussey to consider ways of carrying out the Watson Commission's recommendations. Danquah and several of the older UGCC members agreed to participate in the work of the Coussey Committee, but Nkrumah and his "youngmen" refused to go along with the party leaders. Not only were the committee's members selected in an improper manner, they argued, but the aims of the committee in any case clearly represented a compromise with the principle of "self-government now." On June

12, 1949, Nkrumah announced the formation of a new, more militantly nationalist mass organization, the Convention Peoples' Party (CPP). Kojo Botsio became its secretary, Komlah A. Gbedemah its vice-chairman, and Nkrumah its chairman.

Nkrumah's breach with the UGCC leadership—with such notables as Danquah, Edward Akufo Addo (later President of the Second Republic), William Ofori-Atta, and Kofi A. Busia (an intellectual scion of the Wenchi royal house)—was as much a recognition of differences in political constituencies as it was a dispute over doctrinal or programmatic issues. The old UGCC represented the gradualist viewpoint of the established coastal bourgeoisie, and was bolstered by various traditional rulers who saw a threat to their own interests in the militancy of Nkrumah and his followers. The CPP, on the other hand, spoke to Ghanaians who had been politicized in the immediate post war years: market-women, traders, primary-school leavers, ex-servicemen, journalists, elementary school teachers, urban industrial workers, and clerks in private and government establishments. The more youthful, discontented, and impatient elements of this petty bourgeoisie soon deserted the UGCC in favor of the more activist CPP and its dynamic, attractive young leader, Nkrumah.

The Coussey Committee's report formed the basis of the 1951 Constitution, which set up an Executive Council with a large majority of its ministers to be African, plus an Assembly whose elected members were to be drawn half from towns and rural constituencies and half from traditional councils in the various chiefdoms. Because this Constitution nevertheless fell far short of the CPP's goal of full self-government, Nkrumah and his party launched a protest campaign of "positive action" early in 1950. Strikes, demonstrations, and some violence marked the first months of "positive action" and Nkrumah and his principal lieutenants were arrested and imprisoned for sedition. That move only served to give Nkrumah the status of martyr, as well as to provide added fuel for his movement.

In February 1951, in the first general elections held under the new Constitution, the people elected the Legislative Assembly. Nkrumah, still in jail, carried his own district with a substantial plurality, and the CPP overall gained 34 of the 38 elected seats in the Assembly. With the support of 19 Northern appointed members (i.e., half of the appointed membership), Nkrumah was assured of a working majority. The Governor, Sir Charles Arden-Clarke, immediately released Nkrumah from detention and invited him to form a government as Leader of Government Business, a position similar to Prime Minister, but not quite as prestigious. Nkrumah accepted, and the first CPP government took office on February 26, 1951.

During the next three years, a period marked by cordiality and cooperation between Nkrumah and the British governor, Nkrumah worked to transform the system created by the 1951 Constitution into a full parliamentary government. In 1951 the Assembly acquired a Speaker; in 1952 the position of Prime Minister was created and the Executive Committee became the cabinet. The Prime Minister was made responsible to the Assembly, which confirmed Nkrumah in that office. All these changes were opposed by the traditional elements, particularly by the Ashanti and Northern Territory representatives, who saw in Nkrumah's centralizing efforts an attempt to deprive them of their influence.

Also during this period, the CPP began the process of consolidating its hold over the population and the centers of economic and political power. It organized party branches throughout the country, set up a variety of auxiliary organizations (for youth, women, traders, farmers, etc.), and began to move its people into key positions in various government agencies. For example, by 1953 it had managed to gain control of the Cocoa Purchasing Company (CPC), which had been formed in 1952 as an agency of the Cocoa Marketing Board; an investigation of the CPC in 1956 revealed that the CPP had used the CPC's control of agricultural loans, bulk purchasing, and transportation to enrich the party coffers, to coerce farmers into joining the party, and to control petty commerce that was dependent on cocoa.

In 1954 a new Constitution, written largely at Nkrumah's insistence, ended the election of Assembly members from traditional councils, increased the size of the Assembly (to 104 seats), and stipulated that all Assembly members be chosen from equal-sized, single-member constituencies. The general election of 1954, held under the terms of the new Constitution, confirmed the CPP in office, giving it 72 of the 104 seats in the Assembly. But in addition to underlining the popularity of the CPP's program and Nkrumah's own personal appeal, the election revealed some dissidence within the party and provided an opportunity for opposition in the country's north and center to make itself heard. Shortly after the election, on

September 19, 1954, the first serious challenge to Nkrumah and the CPP was launched in Kumasi with the formation of the National Liberation Movement (NLM). This new party was centered in the Ashanti heartland and was animated by a coalition of Ashanti leaders, both traditional and modern. The NLM leadership also included some CPP dissidents and several former UGCC notables. What is more, it found itself an ally in the Northern Peoples' Party, which had gained fifteen seats in the 1954 elections. The immediate catalyst for the creation of the NLM was a Nkrumah government action that froze prices paid to Ghanaian cocoa producers at levels apparently much below world market prices—and at a time when world prices for the commodity were rapidly rising. The freeze outraged cocoa farmers, most of whom were Ashanti; their revolt was supported by traditional magnates in both the center and the north, many of whom were in any case already angered by the new election rules (which eliminated representation of traditional councils) and by the government's stated policy of whittling down the powers of the chiefs.

The new opposition found articulate spokesmen in the persons of Bafuor Osei Akoto (the principal spokesman—"linguist"—for the Asantehene, paramount chief of the Ashanti), Dr. Kofi A. Busia (a former Professor of Sociology at the University of Ghana who was then MP from Wenchi), and Dr. Danquah. William Ofori-Atta and several influential Ashanti ex-CPP leaders, including Joseph E. Appiah, Reginald R. Amponsah, and Victor Owusu also sided with the new party (the latter two became ministers in Busia's 1969 government). The NLM campaigned for higher cocoa prices, alleged corruption and excesses in the Nkrumah government, and in 1955 after talks for an independence constitution had begun, voiced demands that the new Ghana state be federal rather than unitary in character. The NLM mounted a vigorous campaign in the 1956 elections. It lost to the CPP, which garnered 70 of the 104 seats in the Assembly, but returns showed the CPP margin of popular approval had shrunk to 57 percent of the votes cast.

Following the 1956 election the CPP, armed with a new mandate and a new constitution, asked for and received the grant of Ghanaian independence on March 6, 1957. Meanwhile, the NLM and its allies became the official opposition in the new parliament; they formalized their alliance under the name of the United Party (UP) which was formed in November 1957.

The conditions that precipitated the formation of the NLM in 1954 had not changed appreciably by 1957, and the ruling regime of the new state of Ghana inherited a residue of ill-will and suspicion in the center and north that was to plague it for the rest of its political life. On the other hand, the new country's overall economic situation appeared to be generally healthy; it had inherited a sizable surplus in Cocoa Marketing Board funds, rising cocoa prices had swelled foreign exchange deposits, it had a favorable balance of payments, and most sectors of the economy appeared to be enjoying vigorous economic activity.

During the next three years the regime devoted much of its energies to consolidating its power in the country, emasculating the opposition, and preparing the way for a new republican constitution by which the English institutional and legal constraints (a Governor-General, ministerial government, legalized opposition, an independent judiciary, etc.) could be eliminated or altered in favor of a more centralized, "African socialist" government. Among the various governmental actions to these ends, the following deserve special mention: the Assembly (i.e., the CPP majority) was empowered to amend the Constitution almost at will; the regional assemblies, the last stronghold of traditional power, were abolished; constitutional clauses designed to ensure a competitive and nonpolitical civil service were altered so as to permit Nkrumah to appoint his own followers throughout the upper ranks of government service; the Preventive Detention Act was passed, and by its terms anyone could be held in prison up to five years without being charged (by 1964, an estimated 2,000 people had been held under the Act); and the Deportation Act, came into force, permitting the deportation of persons "disaffected toward the Government of Ghana." On the party front, in 1955 Nkrumah was acclaimed Life Chairman and given the right to choose a majority of the party Central Committee, and in 1956 he gained control over the nomination of candidates to elective office. By 1959 all this, added to the CPP's absolute control over parliament, had created a governing structure that kept the reins of power firmly in the hands of Nkrumah and his closest colleagues.

In April 1960, the regime held a plebiscite to approve a draft republican constitution and to elect Nkrumah as President. The opposition UP had been weakened by defections, detentions, and one exile (Dr. Busia, in 1959); nonetheless it decided to oppose the new constitution and to challenge Nkrumah's candidacy with that of Dr. Danquah. The ensuing campaign was a farce and the plebiscite itself was marred by blatant irregularities: not only was every conceivable obstacle put in the path of Dr. Danquah and his party, but it is clear that miscounting of ballots occurred all over the country. It is also clear that the regime need not have gone to such lengths. Even without electoral manipulation, the vote for the new Constitution, for the Republic, and for Nkrumah undoubtedly would have demonstrated widespread support for both Nkrumah and the regime. As it was, the official count gave Nkrumah and the Republic an implausible 88.5 percent of the total votes cast. Another effect of the plebiscite was a decision to extend the terms of all Assembly incumbents to 1965, it being argued that since the results of the plebiscite amounted to a massive vote of confidence in the regime, new elections to the legislature would amount to a slap in the voters' collective face.

The year 1960 probably marked the apogee of the Nkrumah regime. Thereafter, it found itself increasingly beset by troubles, some the result of its own political and economic mistakes, some instigated by a frustrated opposition, and some fostered by economic factors over which it had little or no control. By 1961 accusations of corruption among the party leadership had grown too loud to be disregarded; moreover, local support for the CPP had eroded as party and government officials found it increasingly difficult to balance the demands for sycophantic loyalty to Nkrumah and the party against the requirements of public service.

This situation gave Nkrumah an opportunity to purge the party leadership of members who had become too critical of his policies. In his celebrated "Dawn Broadcast" of April 8, 1961, Nkrumah denounced official corruption and self-seeking, and shortly thereafter he forced the resignation of several ministers (including Gbedemah). The principal beneficiaries of the purge were more militant leaders of the party, who now saw no impediment to rapid socialist transformation.

Socialist initiatives, however, availed little in the face of a precipitous drop in the world price for cocoa, and in July 1961 the government announced its first austerity budget. Under the impact of increased taxes, forced savings, and a sharp rise in consumer prices, the economy began to sag, a trend abetted by heavy (and often impudent) government commitments to capital spending and widespread misuse of public funds. In September, the dock and railway workers took a long look at the growing shortages, contrasted their own loss of earning power with the visible opulence of the party elite, and went on strike at Sekondi-Takoradi, the country's largest port. When violence broke out, the government responded with force, crushing the strike and arresting and detaining various labor and opposition leaders (including Danquah, Appiah, and Owusu). The suppression of the strike and the detention of the UP leaders did little to quell the discontent or, for that matter, to heal the widening breaches within the party itself. Moreover, when bombs and grenades began to explode in various towns in late 1961 the regime responded with still harsher measures (press censorship, longer detentions, deportations, etc.).

Then, in August 1962, a would-be assassin threw a grenade at Nkrumah while the President was visiting in the village of Kulungugu. With that, Nkrumah turned on his own party radicals. Party Secretary-General Tawia Adamafio, Foreign Affairs Minister Ako Adjei, CPP Executive Secretary Coffie Crabbe, and several other CPP leaders were jailed under the Preventive Detention Act for alleged complicity in the assassination attempt. Adamafio, Adjei, Crabbe and two others were brought to trial in 1963 before a special court for state security cases, created in 1961. The court, composed of Chief Justice Sir Arku Korsah and two other justices of the High Court, Van Lare and Akufo-Addo, acquitted the three principal defendants for lack of evidence. Nkrumah, enraged by the decision, used newly acquired constitutional powers to dismiss Korsah, set aside the verdict, and order re-arrest and re-trial of the defendants. (In 1964, all five were duly retried by a hand-picked court, found guilty, and sentenced to death. Nkrumah commuted their sentences to life imprisonment.)

In the meantime, Nkrumah instituted other moves to consolidate his position. In January 1964 he ordered a referendum on constitutional amendments that would make Ghana officially a one-party state and permit the President to dismiss not merely the Chief Justice but any judge. According to official reports, the proposals passed with 99.9 percent of the voters in favor. In May 1965 parliament so altered the rules governing candidacy for elections that in June of that year, the entire (and unopposed) 118-seat CPP slate was simply declared elected without any polling of voters. The move confirmed what had already been fact for some time: the Ghanaian parliament functioned solely to rubber-stamp the decisions of the President and his colleagues.

Rumors of a coup were already rife in Accra during the summer of 1965, and in July-August of that year Nkrumah moved to reorganize the political side of the military command and to strengthen the defense secretariat. Late in February 1966 the government introduced its new budget which, however, contained little to alleviate popular economic grievances. On February 21, possibly to avoid facing the inevitable protests over his budget, possibly because he genuinely thought he could make a contribution to ending the war in Vietnam, Nkrumah embarked on a trip to Hanoi, via Peking. On February 24, just as he arrived in Peking, a group of military and police officers in Ghana overthrew his regime. Nkrumah went from the Far East to Guinea at the invitation of President Sékou Touré, there to become a nominal co-president of that country and to plan a return to power in Ghana. He died on April 27, 1972, still in exile.

The junta, composed of eight senior army and police officers, styled itself the National Liberation Council (NLC), and immediately began to dismantle the apparatus built by its predecessors. It outlawed the CPP (and indeed, it outlawed all political party activity); it launched a series of investigations into the assets and activities of persons, groups, and agencies in the old regime; and it began trying to unravel the tangle of departments, ministries, agencies, and public corporations whose combined operations during the Nkrumah years had made rational planning and decision-making extraordinarily difficult, if not impossible.

The leaders of the coup—colonels Emmanuel Kotoka, Albert Ocran, and Akwasi A. Afrifa, and Inspector-General of Police John W. Harlley—brought General Joseph Ankrah out of retirement to become Chairman of the NLC. Undoubtedly Ankrah was chosen because he both sympathized with the aims of the coup and projected a desirable father image. He was slow, deliberate, reserved, and, above all, utterly without charisma, a sharp contrast to his flamboyant predecessor. Ankrah gave relatively competent, if unexciting, leadership to the NLC and the country until April 1969, when he was forced to resign following revelations of illegal fund-raising on his behalf. During his tenure, the country had regained much of its political balance, and the groundwork was laid for a return to civilian rule. The NLC had been less successful in dealing with Ghana's economic problems, however. It found itself unable to offset the accumulated indebtedness of the Nkrumah regime, it could not reverse the perennial trade imbalances, and it could do little to ameliorate the chronic malaises of Ghanaian agriculture.

Afrifa became Chairman of the NLC upon Ankrah's resignation, and soon thereafter the NLC published a decree permitting the revival of political parties. By mid-May 1969 a dozen parties had made their appearance. In the meantime, a Constituent Assembly representing a wide range of sectional, ethnic, and economic interests was busy drafting a new constitution. On August 22, 1969, the Constituent Assembly approved, and shortly thereafter, the NLC promulgated the Constitution of the Second Ghanaian Republic. A week later, general elections to a new 140-seat Assembly were held; two main parties and three smaller ones presented a total of 479 candidates to the voters. The Progress Party (PP), led by Dr. Busia and campaigning on what amounted to a "prosperity-and-no-return-to-the-bad-old-days-of-Nkrumah" platform, won 104 seats. The vote for the PP was relatively well distributed throughout the country but most heavily concentrated in the Ashanti center, where Busia's own Ashanti heritage—as well as the overt support of the Ashanti chiefs and that of General Afrifa, also an Ashanti—probably helped his cause a good deal. The principal opposition, the National Alliance of Liberals (NAL), unfortunately permitted itself to be tarred with both a tribal and an Nkrumahist brush (its leader, K. A. Gbedemah, an Ewe, was a former minister in Nkrumah's cabinet), and as a consequence gained only 29 seats, of which 14 were from the Volta Region where the Ewe are the dominant ethnic group.

On September 3, 1969, under the provisions of the new Constitution, Dr. Busia took oath as Prime Minister, and a three-man Presidential Commission (composed of General Afrifa as chairman, Mr. Harlley as vice-chairman, and General Ocran) was also sworn into office. On October 1, 1969, the Second Republic was officially proclaimed.

Since our study deals but marginally with the Busia regime and not at all with its successor, only the briefest of comments about events since 1969 will be made here. The Busia regime had been in power a bare 28 months when, on January 14, 1972, it was in its turn overthrown by a military coup led by Colonel Ignatius K. Acheampong. The new military regime, calling itself the National Redemp-

tion Council (NRC), was still in power at mid-1974, had begun
to tackle Ghana's persistent economic problems with unusual vigor
and determination, and showed little inclination to foster a return of
civilian rule. Part of the NRC's apparent abhorrence of civilian politics undoubtedly lay in the unhappy performance of the Busia
government. An uncomfortable amalgam of long-time foes of
Nkrumah, discards of his regime, and survivors of the political wars of
the 1950s, it proved unable to shift from oppositional politics to the
tasks of ruling a country. In power, Busia and his principal lieutenants
displayed much the same kind of political ineptitude, arrogance,
intolerance of criticism, and enthusiasm for the plusher rewards of
office as they had once so harshly criticized in the Nkrumah regime.
Above all, the Busia government, like the NLC, failed to come to grips
with Ghana's perennial economic problems. Even its bravest efforts to
rescue the economy—devaluation of the currency by nearly 50 percent
in December 1971 and the imposition of stringent and sweeping
financial controls—proved politically unsound, since the resulting
flood of discontent and protest gave the NRC its excuse to intervene.

Finally, for readers who wish to learn more about the political
history of Ghana, the following sources are recommended. The
period from 1946 to 1960 is admirably treated in Dennis Austin,
Politics in Ghana, 1946-1960 (London: Oxford University Press,
1964); of equal value is Nkrumah's own account of his rise to power,
Ghana: The Autobiography of Kwame Nkrumah (New York: Nelson,
1957). An earlier but still useful history of the period before 1957 is
Mother F. M. Bourret, *Ghana, the Road to Independence, 1919-1957*,
rev. ed. (Stanford: Stanford University Press, 1960). A pedestrian but
detailed summary of the 1947-72 period is available in Thomas A.
Howell and Jeffrey P. Rajasooria, eds., *Ghana & Nkrumah* (New
York: Facts on File, Inc., 1972). The more important works on the
1957-66 period are noted earlier in this Introduction (p. xii). For
analysis of the 1966 coup and its causes, see General A. A. Afrifa, *The
Ghana Coup* (London: Frank Cass, 1966), General A. K. Ocran, *A
Myth Is Broken* (Harlow, Essex: Longmans, 1968), and Peter Barker,
(pseud.), *Operation Cold Chop; The Coup That Toppled Nkrumah*
(Accra: Ghana Publishing Company, 1969). The NLM period has
received little attention save in a few articles and scholarly theses; one
of the latter, transformed into a book, is Robert Pinkney, *Ghana*

Under Military Rule, 1966–69 (London: Methuen, 1972). Similarly, the Busia regime has yet to find authoritative chroniclers, but an informative account may be found in David Goldsworthy, "Ghana's Second Republic, a Post-Mortem," *African Affairs* 72, no. 286 (1973): 8–25.

Political Corruption:
An Outline of a Model

Analytic models are among the most useful scholarly tools to help social scientists find their way through the maze of political, social, and economic reality. Without such conceptual maps to guide them, investigators tend to lose their way in tracing complex processual or causal relationships, and to become mired in irrelevancies. The analytical model affords a further advantage in that it does not pretend to serve as a theory, although if carefully constructed it may aid in the development of theory. It is, then, only a topographic sketch of some social or political landscape, and it can easily be adapted and improved as available knowledge increases, or it can be altogether redrawn if the original outline proves misleading.

The present model, which is intended as no more than a preliminary sketch, describes a two-part process in the analysis of political corruption in Ghana. First, it isolates a set of related components that focus on the individual office-holder, his activities, and the matters with which he is concerned ("the core process"). Second, it deals with another set of components, deriving from the first, that operate on the larger system and subsystem levels ("the extended process"). We shall argue that the core process as described in this analysis is applicable to all instances of political corruption in all formal polities, whereas the extended process as described here applies substantially, but not necessarily exclusively, to Ghana.

The core process has five components: political office-holders, political goods, political resources, transaction relationships, and conversion networks. The extended process has two components: a culture of political corruption, and an informal polity. In the discussion to follow, the core process and the extended process are considered in turn by means of a series of definitional propositions that illustrate, clarify, and relate the several components in each set to one another. First, however, our concept of political corruption requires clarification.

Political Corruption

We define political corruption as the unsanctioned, unscheduled use of public political resources and/or goods for private, that is, nonpublic ends. The definition rests on three assumptions: that there is a distinction between "political" and "non-political" corruption; that there is a distinction between "political corruption" and "corruption of process"; and that corruption is a social process.

Throughout this analysis the corruption under discussion is corruption involving the formal polity, embodied in the institutions of government, such as legislatures, executives, courts, bureaucracies, and statutory bodies of various sorts. These institutions operate according to terms set forth in constitutions, statutes, ordinances, decrees, and other written and unwritten rules that have the force of law. The institutions themselves are made up of individual offices, arranged in series, hierarchies, or sets. Whatever the grouping, in each office the occupant functions according to prescriptions and expectations applicable to the office itself. Thus, the term "political" pertains to the structural and human components of the formal polity, and "political corruption" is that corruption which necessarily involves persons who occupy positions in the formal polity. This does not mean that political corruption is restricted to the formal polity in its scope of operation—far from it. Obviously it involves institutions, groups, and persons who deal with the formal polity but are not themselves formally part of its structures. However, unless the acts involve defined members of the formal polity, what is described is not political corruption, but something that might be styled "non-political" corruption.[1]

Our second assumption, concerning the distinction between "political corruption" and another generic type of corruption, "corruption of the political process," rests on two criteria: the relationship of the activity in question to the political process, and the motivation for the activity.

We assume in the case of "political corruption" that office-holders dispose political resources within the framework of ongoing political processes, or at least that they use such processes as bases for the creation and maintenance of corrupt relationships. (In this analysis, political processes are treated as constant and receive only such additional examination as is necessary to clarify some aspect of corrupt transactions.) On the other hand, "corruption of the political process" has as its principal effect the degradation or perversion of the political process. Electoral fraud of various kinds (such as "graveyard registration" and ballot box stuffing), attaining political office under false pretense, suborning perjury, and coercing judges all fall under this rubric.

In "political corruption," more often than not, those involved derive some sort of material benefit. However, personal material gain generally is not a component of "corruption of process." The core of the so-called Watergate Affair in the United States represents an almost pure case of this type of corruption, although it is clear that those involved in the campaign contributions aspect—particularly the big corporate donors—believed or were led to believe that their contributions would lead to governmental preferment. Characteristically, most of the principals—the "insiders" in the government or the Republican party—in that complex of misdeeds sought neither enrichment nor other tangible gain, but such more abstract rewards as political power and the psychic satisfactions of service in a cause and victory over what they believed to be a dangerous enemy.

Admittedly, the line between "political corruption" and "corruption of the political process" may become blurred when the one leads to the other or, as is most often the case, when elements of both may be found in a particular situation. Nevertheless, we make the distinction between the two because it serves to highlight the self-serving behavior that is the central focus of our inquiry.

We also assume that "political corruption" is a social process, that is, a pattern of acts relating at least two actors. Therefore, in this context the corruption of an individual (as suggested in the statement "he is becoming more and more corrupt") is seen either as a consequence of the process or as a particular input into the process that may, for example, increase its scope. Further, to define political corruption as a process does not mean that such a process necessarily constitutes a system. A single, casual two-party corrupt transaction, as for example between a postal clerk and a transient customer, could hardly be called systematic, since the elements of repetition and patterned duration are missing.

With these assumptions in mind, we turn to the elements of our model.

The Core Process

The key to the model is the *individual office-holder* in the formal polity. The functions of the individual occupying a given office or political position are defined not only by the formal, explicit powers and duties attached to the office, but by a political role. The political role is determined by expectations as to how the occupant of a given office ought to behave. Thus, a ministerial secretary, for example, or a constable, not only holds a specific office in a governmental structure, an office that is clearly defined by a schedule of duties; he also plays a role that reflects certain (usually less well defined) expectations about how the job is to be performed. In this sense, the office is a sort of uniform that provides the wearer with explicit and implicit cues about his own expected behavior and also tells others something about how he will probably behave as long as he remains in uniform.

There are several reasons why in this study the crucial element of an office or position is considered to be the individual who occupies it. It is he who represents the linkage between the formal polity and those outside it; it is he who converts political resources into the goods that create, feed, and maintain politically corrupt relationships; and as we shall note in discussing the extended process, it is he who, by converting public (impersonal) resources into private (personal) resources, provides both the capital and the lubricant for the machinations of the "informal polity." Finally, there is a powerful commonsense reason for the centrality of the individual office-holder in this analysis: it is not, after all, institutions or organizations that engage in corrupt political practices,* but people, acting alone or in

---

* In law, to be sure, organizations and institutions may have "legal personality," and are said thereby to assume corporate responsibility, or be held liable for violations of statutory or non-statutory law. My point remains that legal fictions do not "act" in any sociological or political sense.

concert—and in Ghana as elsewhere the practice has been to prosecute individuals, not institutions, for acts of political corruption.

Political goods are those highly desirable things that governments through their agents are in a unique position to dispense.[2] Some may be quite tangible, such as money, electricity, water supplies, roads, jobs, import licenses, food; some are intangible, such as security and protection against external enemies and internal malefactors, information, legitimacy, and access to status and prestige. When Almond and Powell[3] refer to the "distributive capability" of political systems, they are in fact talking about the extent to which governments have the power to dispense political goods. It should be added that the nature (type, quantity, quality) of the political goods to be distributed depends largely on the nature and functions of the state. The more highly centralized the state, the greater the governmental control over economic, social, and political resources, and the greater the quantity—and usually, the value—of the goods distributed. A "constabulary" state, in which public authority plays only a minimal role in economic life, will have fewer political goods to distribute than a welfare state or one with a planned economy.*

Political resources are the official and unofficial capital against which political goods are drawn; to use a banking analogy, as political resources are the deposits, political goods are the currency which office-holders spend in their dealings with one another and with the public. Every political position confers on its occupant access to certain political resources. The nature and relative importance of those resources—and of the goods that can be drawn—are usually defined by the job schedule or set of role-expectations attendant on the position. In this sense, then, what we earlier styled the "uniform" of office can become a political resource (or set of resources) that enables the wearer to trade in certain kinds of political goods.

Political resources and political goods are, as was suggested earlier, either tangible or intangible. Classified according to attribution, there are three main varieties: those related directly to office or position, those related to a political role attached to position, and finally, those attached directly to the person of an office-holder and capable of being used by him independently of the other two. Such personal resources relate to those connected with position and political role to

---

* I am indebted to Drs. Peter Duignan and Lewis Gann for this point.

the extent they are used in conjunction with them. Thus, for example, family connections (a personal resource), when coupled with the influence of position (a role-related resource), may enhance the value of a position-related resource such as facilitation (red-tape cutting, perhaps).

The term *transaction relationships* initially designates the various means by which political resources and goods are used for purposes other than those for which they were originally intended. Terms such as bribery, misappropriation, defalcation, fraud, nepotism, favoritism, are conventionally used to illustrate the ways whereby formal, public political resources find their way into what are essentially private, that is, informal, channels. The conventional use of these terms, however, tends to obscure the *essentially* transactional nature of political corruption and the differences, if any, between criminal acts and political corruption. Each of these matters requires some comment. We argue that a willful act of misappropriation or defalcation, in which an individual, acting alone, takes or uses public property solely for his own benefit, is not an act of political corruption. It becomes a politically corrupt act only when it involves at least two persons, of whom at least one is an office-holder.[4] In either case, of course, the act may be defined by law or regulation as criminal or even as corrupt, and its perpetrator(s) may be subject to penalties. But it is by no means certain that all acts of political corruption are statutorily criminal; for example, flagrant favoritism may be defined as a manifestation of political corruption (by virtue of its necessarily transactional nature) and yet may not be stipulated as criminal behavior in any law or regulation.

For purposes of this analysis, then, a politically corrupt transaction, in its simplest form, involves at least two people, at least one of them acting in an official or quasi-official capacity, in an exchange in which a political good is passed in at least one direction and at least one of the parties knows that the disposition of the political good is unscheduled, illegal, or unsanctioned. The structural ramifications of this basic, two-person transaction are almost endless. They are limited only by the ingenuity of the participants, the purpose(s) of the transaction itself, and the nature of the goods exchanged.[5]

The goods can range over the entire gamut of political resources available to the actors, be they tangible, intangible, position- or role-related, or personal. But whatever their nature, once given, they do not necessarily disappear from the political corruption process, for the single dyadic transaction does not exhaust the life history of the goods themselves. *A* does not simply pass good X to *B*; not even transactions involving tangible goods fit a ball-game metaphor. We consider that all political goods, even the most tangible ones, undergo some degree of transformation as they are distributed and used, and may in fact lose their identities along the way. That transformation, which occurs or begins to occur when the goods reach the hands of the first recipient, is here termed *conversion*, and the channels through which the goods subsequently travel constitute the *conversion network*. Theoretically, it should be possible to follow the conversion of political goods as they are passed on, broken up, passed on further, changed again, much as scientists can trace irradiated particles through living bodies. Actually, given the range of potential recipients in the conversion network and the mutable and often intangible nature of the goods, precise tracking at all points is generally either hopeless or impractical. But we can say with confidence that conversion does take place and under the right circumstance it can be traced. An example may clarify the point:

Assume *B* pays official *A* a bribe—a sum of money—to do him a service. It need hardly be pointed out that after *A* takes the money his options in spending it are almost infinite. But assume he chooses to apply the whole sum directly to the purchase of an automobile. Here is a clear conversion trace. Let us now focus on the other side of the transaction—on the service *A* renders *B*. It can be argued that that service (a political good) also leaves an identifiable conversion trace. Assume that the service in question is an introduction of *B* to *R*, an influential man who can help *B* make a substantial profit. In this instance, an act of facilitation is converted into a potentially valuable entrée.

The Extended Process

The extended process of political corruption, to recapitulate, includes two principal components, the culture of political corruption, and the informal polity. Both of these components (in contrast to the components of the core process) tend to operate on the larger subsystem or system levels; both exist as outgrowths of an expanded and generalized core process. We also argue that an informal polity cannot develop in the absence of a culture of political corruption, but a culture of political corruption can exist without an informal polity.

The culture of political corruption. A political culture, as defined by Almond and Verba and by Dawson and Prewitt, among others, is determined in part by operative political values, orientations, and attitudes and their related practices, as well as by the formalized behaviors and structures that go into the maintenance of a political system.[6] The definitions formulated by these scholars vary in some respects, but all agree that the key component of a political culture is the body of orientations, attitudes, and values that yield criteria for determining what is politically legitimate and what is not. Some have also argued, as has the author, that a political system may contain more than one political culture,[7] and out of the interaction of diverse political cultures within the system, the prevailing criteria of political legitimacy may change.

Thus, for example, the use of violence as a means of achieving political ends, such as changing governments, may emerge and become so institutionalized that we may even speak of a political "culture of violence."[8] By analogy and extension, when politically corrupt transactions become so pervasive in a political system that they are the *expected norm* in transactions involving government officials, a culture of political corruption can be said to exist.

The existence of a culture of political corruption may be inferred in part where it is overtly clear that a large number of politically corrupt transactions are taking place (*how* large a number is another problem). Beyond that, once politically corrupt transactions become commonplace it is unlikely that they will in all cases remain confined to two persons. We argue that politically corrupt relationships tend to spread, and to ramify into increasingly complex networks of personal involvement through which political goods flow. And the visibility and complexity of these networks affords some measure of the extent and depth of the culture of political corruption.[9]

The informal polity. In our discussion of the core process, we have demonstrated how by means of a corrupt political transaction political goods pass into the conversion network, and we have suggested how they may move into a ramified set of relationships beyond the simple dyadic transaction. When these ramified relationships become systematized (i.e., when the elements of repetition and patterned duration are present), they constitute what we shall term "informal political networks." These are relationships based on various kinds of interpersonal links such as "old boy" ties (for example in Ghana, the "brotherhood" of graduates of Achimota and other exclusive secondary schools); friendship; family, clan, or ethnic affinities; patronage or clientilistic reciprocities; or business obligations. Their common characteristic is *informality*; that is, they normally lie outside the formal polity in the sense that they are not *defined* as part of the institutional network of positions and roles. They share with the formal polity, first, those individuals who function *both* as part of the formal polity and as part of the informal networks, and second, access (directly or indirectly) to political resources.

Informal political networks need not, of course, exist principally outside official structures; quite often they are established within official structures and most of the persons involved may hold positions within the polity (it should be added, however, that in Ghana such networks commonly involve more people outside the polity than within). The salient point is that by definition the informal political networks *themselves* lie beyond the official pale, and the distribution and conversion of political goods constituting their *raison d'être* is unsanctioned, illicit, or at best morally unacceptable.

When informal political networks become so well established within the political system that their activities and influence begin to parallel those of governmental structures, they constitute an *informal polity*. The point at which informal political networks become informal polities may, in fact, define the boundary between what some scholars have called *political* and *parapolitical* systems.[10] By the time the informal polity develops, political corruption is already so widespread that a culture of political corruption clearly exists as a prior condition.

What is here called the informal polity is difficult to describe precisely because, unlike the formal polity, it tends to be structurally amorphous and constantly changing. Whereas the formal polity has defined hierarchies of office and role, the informal polity exists in large part to bypass established chains of command and, in effect, to operate in the interstices between government structures. Whereas the formal polity defines the norms and limitations appropriate to each (political) position, the network of relationships in the informal polity functions on a largely pragmatic, ad hoc basis. Whereas the formal polity seeks to operate with as much continuity and predictability as possible, relationships within the informal polity tend to change as available resources change, political positions shift, and office-holders move up, down, laterally, or out. (In Ghana, for example, the "verandah boys," so called because they could be seen ostentatiously lounging about on the verandahs and porches outside the offices of "big men," tended to be somewhat fickle, switching allegiances when the fortunes of their patrons waned.)

The informal polity does, however, assume shape and visible structure as it grows. The more extensive its supporting networks, the more pervasive the political culture of corruption, the more highly crystallized—and enduring—the informal polity becomes. Whether an informal polity merely exists in symbiosis with the formal polity, or whether it becomes a parasitic or even takes over its host is a question that can be answered only in relation to a real situation.[11]

We have suggested earlier that a given political system might in fact contain not one but several political cultures. It is also demonstrable that political systems are usually themselves composed of several political subsystems. Thus, there is the distinct possibility that a political system may contain several informal polities, each related to one or more subsystems. Again, of course, whether or not a plurality of informal polities actually exists within a given political system becomes an empirical question; yet it is almost implicit where a culture of political corruption pervades a national political system that encompasses regional and other parochial subsystems.[12]

The concept of the "informal polity" is susceptible to yet further development. We have posited the "informal polity" as a relatively amorphous system intersecting the formal polity at points at which officials enter into networks of corrupt relationships, but one which nonetheless maintains a separate identity. Logically, the distinctions between the formal and informal polities can become so blurred the two seem as one; when this occurs, political corruption achieves near-official sanction. John Waterbury argues that this has occurred in Morocco, where what he calls "free-floating, endemic corruption" not only mirrors a thoroughgoing culture of political corruption but appears to be an expression of the preferred way of doing political business. According to Waterbury:

> As the case of Morocco would tend to demonstrate, corruption is not simply an aspect of politics but has displaced and dwarfed all other

forms of politics. Thus, in Morocco, free-floating corruption is manipulated, guided, planned, and desired by the regime itself.[13]

Waterbury argues that the patrimonial nature of the Moroccan regime, a "parallel, non-official, and illegal system of payments and incentives,"[14] a finely honed spoils system, and a calculated policy of keeping politicians and officials insecure, have all contributed to the development of this "planned, endemic corruption." Whatever the causes, Waterbury's account clearly shows that Morocco has developed both a culture of political corruption and an informal polity. Although Ghana during the period under study had not attained the extremes of the Moroccan example, the Moroccan example is particularly instructive to our analysis as it suggests what can happen to a political system in which political corruption is permitted to grow unchecked.

2

The Culture of Political Corruption

It would be idle to ignore the existence of bribery and corruption in many walks of life in the Gold Coast admitted to us by every responsible African to whom we addressed the question. That it may spread as further responsibility devolves upon the African is a possibility which cannot be denied.

Watson Commission, 1948[1]

Massive material corruption seems to have taken hold of the new class of (West) African politicians and their followers since they began to come into power. It is so widespread as to be universal, at least in this area.

Legon Observer, 1966[2]

In 1969, it was reliably reported that a quarter of all Ghana's consumption of cigarettes was satisfied by smuggling. . . . On top of that, a third of all drugs and supplies of the Ministry of Health are, at a conservative estimate, stolen or diverted. Were it not for the laws of libel, it would be very easy to give much more concrete and impressive evidence of the importance of corruption in Ghana.

M. J. Sharpston, 1970[3]

We Ghanaians are so accustomed to bribing our officials, and they to stealing our rate-moneys, that it would be considered odd if we didn't bribe and they didn't steal.

Mr. J., former Ghanaian official, 1971[4]

The above quotation from the report of the Watson Commission shows that as early as 1948 political corruption was seen by some Ghanaian observers as a cause for concern. The other quotations, taken together, attest to a commonly held view that by the end of the 1960s Ghana had developed what we term a culture of political corruption. It had been a long time in the making, but by then its outlines were unmistakable. Bribery, graft, nepotism, favoritism, and the like had become commonplace at all levels of officialdom; and what is more, much of the public had come to expect officials to conduct their business in a spirit of subterfuge, dishonesty, and mendacity on all sides.

The views expressed in these quotations suggest that Ghanaian political corruption in the 1960s might have reached a scale and pervasiveness comparable to Indonesia under Sukarno (1958–65), and to Haiti and the Philippines today. James C. Scott pungently outlines the situation in Sukarno's Indonesia in his comparative study of political corruption: "Corruption was common in Indonesia under parliamentary cabinet rule, but under Guided Democracy [1958–65] it attained truly epidemic proportions."[5] At the highest echelons, "A powerful group of 'palace millionaires' . . . emerged. Their methods included bribing for state-guaranteed economic privileges and for protection of their black market sales, lavish gifts to ministers, conspiring with bureaucrats in the falsification of accounts and inventories, and a variety of other corrupt practices designed to assure profit with safety."[6] These were the businessmen; they had their counterpart in governmental ranks in what Scott calls "the bureaucratic-military cliques." Further, "both low and high-ranking officials extracted what profit they could from their positions. Their own salaries greatly eroded by inflation, officials extorted payments for expediting a claimant's case, for issuing necessary permits and licenses, for arranging an appointment with a superior—in short, for any service that was of value to citizens."[7] Scott points out that the Indonesian case was distinctive for "the total volume of corruption and the absence of any limits."[8]

In present-day Haiti (also discussed by Scott) an all-pervasive corruption is combined with terrorism to serve the will of a self-perpetuating oligarchy of indigenous political entrepreneurs.[9] In the Philippines, although corruption has reached its extremes in the electoral process (i.e., in a form of what we term "corruption of the political process"), the extraordinary excesses connected with this abuse have had sufficient ramifications throughout the system[10] to create a culture of political corruption. Finally, if an example closer to Ghana is sought, then by all accounts Western Nigeria—at least between 1964 and 1966—achieved something close to a culture of political corruption; according to Stanislas Andreski, the region in that period became a "kleptocracy," that is, a political system ruled by thieves.[11]

But has Ghanaian corruption ever really gone so far? In 1966 at least one Ghanaian intellectual, a lecturer at the University of Ghana, was prepared to render summary judgment in the affirmative:

> This whole society is corrupt: corruption for us is a way of life. Everyone from the big man down to the small is out to get his, and a people who have had little in the past will take advantage of opportunities with a feeling of "why shouldn't we as long as no one gets directly hurt."[12]

The statement may, of course, have been inspired mainly by first-flush reaction to the post-coup revelations, which by mid-1966 were beginning to capture widespread attention. In contrast, a number of sober students of Ghanaian politics and society have argued that corruption in Ghana in the Nkrumah era was neither as pervasive nor as ultimately destructive to Ghana's politics and economy as the popular image would suggest. Beverley J. Pooley, an Anglo-American legal scholar, asserts that the evidence of the post-coup Commissions of Inquiry permits the limited conclusion that "corruption at the topmost level . . . was amply proved." Beyond that, although "relatively low-level corruption certainly existed . . . the serious financial difficulties of the country and of the enterprises under investigation were due to a much larger extent to inefficiency, poor administration, and the lack of clear directives than they were to outright corruption."[13] Scott concludes that political corruption in Ghana was more prevalent among the ethnic "ins" (groups favored by the Nkrumah regime) than among those relatively disadvantaged by the regime (such as the Ashanti, who were identified with a political party that opposed Nkrumah in the early 1950s).[14] Peter Omari implies that corruption in Ghana was largely an elite phenomenon,[15] and Henry Bretton's study of "personal rule" in Ghana tends toward a similar conclusion.[16]

In the face of such contradictory estimates, it may be pertinent to re-examine the evidence from a fresh perspective. Let us assume the possibility of a culture of political corruption, and then examine the question of what would constitute adequate evidence of its existence. At first glance, it might seem the ideal situation would be to demonstrate conclusively and in quantitative terms that politically corrupt transactions in a given system are the rule rather than the exception,

that significantly more than half of the total volume of official transactions in that system over a given period of time are politically
corrupt. Unfortunately, the requisite data in most cases are not available to enable such an analysis, and even if they were, the sheer
volume of official transactions in any but the most primitive system
would pose staggering problems of tabulation and interpretation.
Moreover, there is of course more to a culture of political corruption
than can be expressed in simple quantitative terms. Such a culture
embodies certain supportive values, orientations, and expectations
that not only affect the scope of corruption but determine its focus
(i.e., for example, who should be bribed) and its modus operandi (e.g.,
how and when a transaction ought to be initiated and how much it
should cost). Thus it is more than likely, even perhaps both necessary
and desirable, that "proof" of a culture of political corruption consists
of a compound of data—published documentation, personal intui-
tions and observations, the cumulative observations and judgments of
others, and a wide range of circumstantial evidence. Undeniably, such
evidence is likely to be empirically deficient in many respects; however if it can be compared against an example that might convincingly
be termed an "ideal type" (such as the Indonesian case), its dimensions might become more visible.

With these qualifications in mind, turning again to Ghana, it is
possible to assert that the outlines and some of the substance of a
culture of political corruption were visible there by 1970, although
Ghana was still light years away from the Indonesian "ideal." The
supporting evidence can be most readily grouped under three rubrics:
(1) data concerning the growth of political corruption between 1938
and 1966, (2) data emerging from the post-coup revelations, and (3)
data concerning corruption during the National Liberation Council
and Busia periods (1966–69, 1969–72). The last category includes
first-hand observations and other evidence gathered by the author
between 1969 and 1971.

The Growth of Political Corruption between 1938 and 1966

Most of the data published up to 1966 on political corruption in
Ghana is circumstantial and secondary in nature, but it is nevertheless
sufficiently detailed to permit strong inferences to be made. The most

reliable sources are the reports of several Commissions of Inquiry, parliamentary documents, and, most useful for our purposes, the series of reports by the principal auditors of governmental accounts, first for the Gold Coast Colony and later for Ghana during the Nkrumah and National Liberation Council periods. Publication of the audit reports actually began around the turn of the century, but the author was able to inspect only those covering the 31-year period between 1939 and 1969.[17] These reports are the work of only three civil servants, two British and one Ghanaian; the Ghanaian, Auditor-General Ahenkora Osei, took over the audits in 1963 and in fact retained his position through 1971, long after most high officials from Nkrumah's regime had been dismissed. There is a notable continuity in the audits, not only in format but in style of expression (which tends to be dry) and in the fact that all three compilers were clearly scrupulous in the pursuit of their duties. All three condemned over-spending, wasteful practices, financial irregularities, and willful extravagance with government funds without regard to whether these abuses were practiced by Englishmen or by Ghanaians. Testimony to Osei's probity can be seen in his long tenure and in the tone of his reports covering the later years of the Nkrumah period, when the regime's financial profligacy appears to have been at its height. During that period Osei even permitted himself occasional expressions of carefully modulated exasperation when his warnings and queries were repeatedly disregarded.

Granting that the audit reports cover only the highlights of *central* government responsibility, that they are based on information pulled together by undermanned staffs, that their commentary tends to be terse (often necessitating reading between the lines), and that they were undoubtedly affected at times by poor (or even suborned[18]) field audits, they nevertheless record an unmistakable pattern of increasing corruption over the years. What is more, for whatever reasons, this increase appears to correspond to the increased Ghanaization of the civil service and government at least until 1956.

Between 1938 and 1943, the audit reports single out no notable cases of fraud, theft, or other irregularity, although increased pilferage of government stores is noted. Then, in the 1943-44 report, the first itemization of "irregularities" appears: 31 cases, involving amounts from £3 to £6,500. The £6,500 item represents various losses incurred by the Medical Department, largely through looting and theft of payments vouchers. Of the other cases, at least 20 are attributed to misappropriations, defalcations, thefts, and frauds perpetrated by officials—carrying the strong implication that political corruption was involved.

The 1944–45 report lists 26 cases (of which 16 are possible instances of corruption); the 1945–46 report comments on the "not inconsiderable" number of frauds and irregularities but provides no list; the 1946–47 report lists 37 cases (of which at least 20 are possible cases of corruption); and by 1950–51 the list has grown to 152 cases, of which perhaps 88 can be attributed to corrupt acts. In the 1950–51 report the Director of Audit makes one of his characteristically understated observations concerning that year's situation: "The types of fraud perpetrated were more frequent in occurrence but in general of a similar nature to those reported in previous years. The magnitude of the losses in the case of the Public Works Department's cash and stores and in the case of fraudulent withdrawals from the Post Office Savings Bank is a matter of considerable concern."[19] By 1951, also, the Watson Commission had submitted its report, which not only contained an ominous warning about future corruption but concluded that the prevailing system of retail and wholesale trade had led to "great abuses and encouraged bribery and excessive charges."[20]

The 1953–54 audit report presented what it styled a "formidable" list of 230 cases and deplored the mounting incidence of fraud and other irregularities in the Public Works, Post Office, and Health departments; about 150 of the cases for that year appear to represent corrupt acts. By 1954–55 the incidence of fiscal irregularity had grown to such proportions that the list was now limited to cases involving cash losses greater than £ 10 and losses of stores worth more than £ 25. The auditor's comments once again were to the point: "The steadily increasing number of loss cases presents a most serious problem to Government. . . . [It] is also a disturbing reflection on present standards and underlines the absence of adequate experienced supervisory staff."[21] About 85 of the 130 cases listed for that year could be attributed to corrupt practices.

A factor that probably contributed as much as any other to the increased incidence and generalization of corruption in the 1950s bears mention at this point: the growth of state corporations and marketing boards. The marketing boards came into being in 1947 with the establishment of the Gold Coast Cocoa Marketing Board,

and in 1949 the Gold Coast Agricultural Products Marketing Board
was created. Both were to expand their activities in the years ahead,
and to carry over into the post-independence system. State corporations, secretariats, commissions, authorities, and the like, proliferated
throughout the system after independence, that is, after 1957, in
response to the increasing numbers of specialized functions assigned
the central government bureaucracy. The relationship between state
corporations and their auxiliary institutions and the growth of political corruption is discussed at length later in this chapter; suffice it for
the present to note that they provided almost unlimited opportunities
for the diversion of public goods to favorably placed entrepreneurs at
all levels both within and without the formal polity.

As for the marketing boards, from their very inception they almost
certainly expanded political corruption at the lower levels of officialdom. During the colonial period, British and Ghanaian officials in the
top echelons of the boards' administration stood to gain little from
corrupt practices because the bureaucratic norms to which they
adhered imposed severe social and practical sanctions on those so
involved. At the lower echelons, however, where the bulk of the
boards' work was carried on—in purchasing, weighing, bagging,
transport, etc.—the situation was different. Here, boards' agents had
to deal not only with individual farmers and petty entrepreneurs, but
with a wide variety of local farmers' associations,[22] as well as with
cartels of market-women, transporters, petty traders, and wholesalers.
Many of these individuals and groups had been operating for some
time, and some had succeeded in monopolizing markets in primary
commodities by the time the boards came into being. Obviously these
persons and groups were loath to surrender their control over the
market. When they discovered they could not effectively compete
with state marketing cartels, they resorted to manipulating the boards'
grass-roots activities.[23] Thus even before Nkrumah's regime, collusory
and manipulative dealings in the marketing boards were already
widespread and large amounts of money were involved.

It is hardly surprising that when the Convention People's Party
came to power it cast a covetous eye at the marketing boards; such a
lucrative source of revenue could scarcely be ignored. Between 1952
and 1954 the party sought and gained control of the Cocoa Purchasing
Company, a subsidiary of the Cocoa Marketing Board and a key state
marketing agency. One of the most important functions of the CPC

was to provide loans to cocoa farmers; party control of the CPC meant that loans became a form of political patronage, and that only farmers willing to pledge both loyalty and "contributions" to the CPP could obtain them. With this move, the CPP in effect took over from the Cocoa Marketing Board the unobtrusive but important function of fleecing the peasants for the benefit of the emerging middle class. The party was now in a position to bring its coercive capabilities to bear on recalcitrant farmers' groups and, in the bargain, to acquire access to an almost unlimited source of funds.[24] The more general effect, the increased scope of state activity and its relationship to the growth of political corruption, is well described by John Waterbury:

> The poor of the Third World may have exchanged one kind of vulnerability for another. The introduction of Mexican wheat may lead to increased yields, but the peasant must somehow obtain credit from the state agricultural credit bank and hope for the best in a market pricing system partially or totally determined by the state. The need for intercessors, protectors, and patrons is no less now than it was in the past. Moreover, the contemporary power and penetration of the modern state apparatus has in many instances been achieved without any modification of the degree of real or perceived material scarcity. Competition for privileged access to state services or relief from impositions has come to dominate political life; the scope for corrupt patronage has expanded with the state itself.[25]

On March 6, 1957, Ghana became independent. The new regime inherited a large foreign exchange balance, a sizable budgetary surplus, a relatively efficient economy, and a windfall in tax revenues, which had come to about 30 percent above estimates because of changes in the structure of the tax system. The 1955–56 auditor's report, which was published almost coincidentally with the celebration of independence, sounded what may have been the only jarring note on that occasion; however, there is no evidence that people paid much attention to it. Once again, the auditor-general commented on the financial irresponsibility of the nation's rulers:

> The habit of liberality with Government funds, acquired during this period of buoyant revenue, is difficult to reverse whilst the formidable list of losses and frauds gives a disquieting commentary on standards of integrity.

Difficulty has been experienced in relating claims for expenses incurred overseas by Ministers and other representatives of Government to the scales approved by Finance Committee.[26]

Leading the lists of big spenders was Prime Minister Nkrumah, who had exceeded official budget by 200 percent. The annual list of irregularities cited 156 cases, of which more than half appear to be instances of corruption. Losses ran up to £ 45,000, not including, as the auditor pointed out, undisclosed losses or losses by district and municipal councils (audits on the finances of local governmental units were relatively infrequent and poorly conducted, and often remained unpublished for a variety of reasons). The 1957–58 report, covering the first year of independence, contained this more restrained but still pointed comment: "The scale of losses continues to give cause for concern...."[27] The list for that year included 202 cases, of which, again, over half could be attributed to corrupt dealings; total losses now amounted to about £ G78,000.

By 1961 the annual auditor-general's report had begun to read like a veritable catalogue of financial mismanagement and irregularity. The 1960–61 report, published in 1962, reported large-scale defaults on loans, and the failures and liquidations of at least six government corporations. It also gave a foretaste of the findings that were to emerge from the Commissions of Inquiry after the 1966 coup. It included for comment such matters as proliferating travel allowances and mileage claims, excessive drawing on amenity and family allowances, widespread unauthorized bookings of passage to England (for families of officials), overpayment on contracts (12 such cases are noted), inflated building contract estimates, and too-frequent purchase abroad of expensive goods available more cheaply in Ghana (specifically, the report notes a £ G100,402 Defense Ministry purchase of furniture from England. "The purchase of expensive carpets for use in offices," notes the report, "has become increasingly common. In one instance a number were purchased and the payment charged to 'Election Expenses.' " The Ministry of Foreign Affairs in particular is criticized for its financial profligacy; it appears not only to have "abused its privileges" in general, but to have increased representational allowances without authorization, taken on much redundant staff, and permitted excessive payments for medical care, air travel, communications, local transportation (the London High

Commission alone, the most free-wheeling of the missions, had reported expenditures of £ G18,735 *in four months* on taxis and automobile rentals). The missions also commonly overdrew on their allowances and paid enormous sums for accommodations—one mission paid £ G104,716 for an apartment in Paris and another £ G12,000 for an apartment in Accra. In sum, the report concludes drily, the missions displayed "a disregard for economy in administering their day-to-day affairs."[28] Beside these matters, the rest of the 1960-61 list of abuses, totaling 158 cases and over £ G107,559 in losses, seems insignificant; about 87 of these cases appear to involve corrupt acts. Finally, the same report makes mention of an unresolved matter of £ G210,230 in fraudulent grant payments made in 1959-60 in connection with an agricultural scheme at Suhum.

The 1961-62 and 1962-63 reports reveal the same pattern, but with the picture more somber than before. Again, overspending and questionable practices are everywhere in evidence, and the lists of frauds and other irregularities cite total losses topping the £ G600,000 mark. Corrupt practices and financial maladministration in state corporations and boards now begin to come to light in the audits; and again the unchecked financial irresponsibility in Foreign Ministry draws acerb comment: "In keeping with past practice, Missions have continued to spend extravagantly at the least opportunity."[29] The Ghanaian Embassy in Washington, D. C., in that period negotiated to pay £ G214,000 for a building previously rejected by the Indian Mission on an architect's advice that it was too old for effective repairs (subsequent investigation, reported in 1966, revealed that this entire transaction was shot through with corrupt practices[30]). In all, 29 of the 56 gazetted diplomatic missions overspent their estimates between 1961 and 1963, and their personnel in the same period were involved in a wide range of illicit and corrupt dealing. Some of these dealings involved fairly large sums of money (for example, the auditors queried a four-month expenditure of £ G17,328 for telegrams charged to the London Mission); others exemplified petty mendacity in the extreme (one ambassador charged his mission for the rental of his personal typewriter). In other incidents, one diplomat authorized the purchase of a bouquet and a coffin at government expense for a deceased relative, and still another rewarded his wife's pregnancy with a generous and totally illegal cash allowance.

Concern over the mounting costs of financial mismanagement

and political corruption was not limited to the Auditor-General's Department, nor was scrutiny always confined to the activities of the central government. Even staunch supporters of the government on occasion expressed dismay at the extent to which corruption had spread throughout the system. Notable in this respect were the members of the Public Accounts Committee of the National Assembly, who took their role as watchdogs of the public purse quite seriously. The following two statements are from the published debates on the Committee's report during the 1963–64 parliamentary session; the first exemplifies the frequent irritation expressed by Committee members, and the second reflects a rarer, but nonetheless genuine, outrage:

[Mr. I. J. Adomako-Mensah, commenting on fraudulent expenditures by the Ho Urban Council]. Here, in Ghana, when men want to misappropriate funds, they try to do so in a clever way. They invent something plausible to do with the money; they invent projects and activities and then they are able to take for themselves their concealed quota. . . . We know enough of these things. What does the Regional Organization say to another diversion of £ G3,477 18s 1d. to construct a rest house at Kpedze? It is another admitted irregularity. Then £ G2,000 meant for bungalow approaches and drives was was also fraudulently used on a private club-house which is no Government project. May the Accountant-General and the Auditor-General save the country from such acts.[31]

[Mr. B. E. Kusi, commenting on some £ G150,000 for which the Ghana Educational Trust could not account]. We here are the caretakers of national funds and it is our duty to see that those people who have charge of this money should account for any loss. Are we to sit down and look on when those people in charge of the money are unable to account for no less than £ G150,000? The President, in the Government's policy statement, told us recently that they were going all out to provide free secondary education for our children; and they will inevitably put money into the hands of some of us to carry out the policy. If no exemplary action is taken now in respect to those who have misused the sum of £ G150,000, it is likely that anybody who will be trusted with money in the future to carry out the government's educational policy will put that money in his pocket. If no action is taken to bring those concerned to book, I will not take the Government serious [sic] and I will not take the statement of the President seriously. Many children go about in the streets because they cannot get accommodation in secondary schools, while those who have charge of the money send their children to international schools and to universities. Most of them ride in *Mercedes Benz* 220[s] and yet call themselves socialists. This is very bad. If we want to build a socialist country, then we must let the President know that we are serious about the use of public funds and that we do not pay mere lip-service to socialism.[32]

For all its sense of public conscience, however, the Public Accounts Committee seldom, if ever, looked into the politically dangerous areas of the Presidency, the party, and the activities of the country's ministerial oligarchs. For one thing, powerful individuals like Kofi Baako, minister of information, were always on hand to see that the Committee kept its probes limited; for another, it is clear, as Henry Bretton suggests, that its "detection devices were most delicately attuned to avoid setting off political dynamite."[33]

There is nothing to indicate that a similar charge could be laid at the door of the Auditor-General, but it is obvious that certain government agencies permitted only limited audit or remained closed to audit altogether. For example, the disposal of the President's contingency fund (nearly ₵5,000,000 during 1965) was not scrutinized, nor were the expenditures of the Bureau of African Affairs (BAA) and the Winneba Ideological Institute. (These two agencies operated on both overt and covert levels; the BAA, for example, helped finance and train guerrillas for operations in other African countries, and the Winneba Institute conducted training in Nkrumahist thought and in political warfare. Clearly, open audits on these agencies might be extremely embarrassing to the regime.) Given the circumstances, it is quite remarkable that the Auditor-General's Department revealed as much as it did, for clearly prudence dictated that it exercise restraint.

Sometimes, however, a public scandal could not be kept quiet, or corruption in high places attracted such notoriety that some public action had to be taken, or a problem fed by widespread corruption became so aggravated that it was politically dangerous for the government to remain silent. In such cases, official reaction might take the form of a commission of inquiry, but in extreme cases Nkrumah himself intervened. Five instances of official intervention are particularly instructive for what they reveal of the nature of such inquiries: the celebrated "Braimah case" (1953), the Cocoa Purchasing Company scandals (1955-56), the import licenses racket (1963-65), the trade malpractices investigation (1965), and the series of events surrounding Nkrumah's "Dawn Broadcast" (April 8, 1961).[34]

The "Braimah case" centered about J. A. Braimah, who was one of the ministers in Nkrumah's 1950 government. He resigned in 1953 after allegations of bribery and corruption were made against him; specifically, he was charged with accepting £ 2,000 "for election expenses" from an Armenian contractor. At the same time, various other charges were leveled against other officials, one being the allegation that Prime Minister Nkrumah himself had borrowed £ 1,800 from A. Y. K. Djin, then the CPP Finance Committee chairman, and that the loan had been made through Ohene Djan, a ministerial secretary, to pay for the importation of a Cadillac automobile. An investigating commission headed by Sir Arku Korsah finally concluded that most of the allegations against high officeholders in this case were unsubstantiated; nevertheless, as a result of evidence submitted to the commission Braimah was not re-instated, and Ohene Djan and some other lesser officials were sent to prison.

A series of scandals involving the Cocoa Purchasing Company (CPC) surfaced three years later. Among other allegations that led to this investigation was a charge that funds of the CPC, a semi-governmental body, had been appropriated "for political purposes," that is, for use by the CPP. A Commission of Inquiry headed by Olumuyiwa Jibowu found that the CPC was indeed "controlled by the CPP" and that the funds in question had been applied "for the purpose of winning adherents for the CPP" by the device of granting loans mainly to "party sympathizers." Further, the commission found that some CPC officials had been involved in bribery, extortion, and other acts of corruption, and that the CPC managing director had used his office both for private gain and for the benefit of the CPP. The CPC managing director was A. Y. K. Djin, the CPP Finance Committee chairman whose name had arisen in connection with the "Braimah case." The Jibowu Commission delicately sidestepped all allegations of financial connection between Djin and Nkrumah, but left the strong impression that Nkrumah had, at the very least, been imprudent in his dealings with Djin and the CPC.[35] Djin was dismissed from his CPC position, but not from the party; he later became minister of trade, but was finally dropped from the government in 1965 when he was once again implicated in high-level fraud.

By 1963 it was evident that the once prosperous Ghanaian economy had begun to falter badly, and even more disturbing, it was widely held that extensive political corruption had played a role in bringing about this state of affairs. Having presumably cleansed its topmost levels in 1961 (at the time of the Dawn Broadcast), the government could now "reveal the role that many lower-level functionaries and foreign companies played in undermining the economy." The exposures of corruption in import licensing in 1964 and the formation of the Abraham Commission on Trade Malpractices in 1965 appear in retrospect to have represented two government attempts to find scapegoats for its own policy failures.

The import license racket, which implicated the Chief of the (Police) Criminal Investigation Division as well as a number of other functionaries and a variety of Indian, Levantine, and African merchants, seemed relatively unimportant at the time in terms of scope and substance: the report issued by the investigating Akainyah Commission indicated that the sums involved were not very large. In light of the post-Nkrumah revelations concerning import licensing corruption,[36] however, it could be argued that the commission either chose to report only enough evidence to allay public apprehensions, or it willfully closed its eyes to the true dimensions of the problem. In any case, the Akainayah Commission in 1964 expressed confidence that its very appointment had "operated as a stop-cork on the import license racket" and concluded its report with this pious pronouncement:

> It is unfortunate and pathetic that the love of money has become an obsession with some of us, and drives us to any length to get rich quick without stopping to think of the consequences. So long as we can get the money, we do not care whether or not our country is plunged into bankruptcy.[37]

Unfortunately for the cause of official credibility, Justice Akainyah himself was subsequently caught up in an investigation concerning import licenses.[38] Nor was this all; the Ollenu Commission, appointed after the 1966 coup, pointed out that the third chapter of the Akainyah report (which was to have discussed "substantiated" allegations of bribery and corruption in the Ministry of Trade) was never published,[39] apparently because it contained information that would have been embarrassing to highly placed individuals in the government.

The 1965 Abraham Report on Trade Malpractices was similarly censored before publication,[40] but even in its expurgated version it presents an extraordinary picture of maladministration and political corruption (in our terms) at the middle and lower levels of Ghanaian officialdom. Stated briefly, the Abraham Commission was charged primarily to investigate the system of wholesale and retail trade in Ghana and to determine the "pattern, causes, and occasion of difficulties encountered by the general public in the purchase of goods." Its findings touched upon import license procedures (which were identified as a major cause of shortages and high prices), local food production (here underproduction was condemned, along with the activities of the State Farms Corporation and of foreign importers), manufacturers (including certain state-owned corporations whose production activities were deemed highly questionable), the commodity distribution system (including, notably, the Ghana National Trading Company [GNTC], whose manifold importing, wholesaling, and retailing activities came in for much detailed criticism), petty traders (including some 20,000 pass-book traders, many of whom had preferential access to retail and wholesale commodities), conditional sales (a widespread practice of "you may have this only if you buy that" was roundly condemned), the pricing system, and the general quality of administration at all levels of the economy. In its final sections, the Abraham report named no less than 49 officials in the GNTC, three in the Ghana National Construction Corporation (GNCC), two in the Ministry of Trade, two in private companies, and two in the State Fisheries Corporation "whose activities do not ... help the success of the ... organizations they represent."[41] Detailed comments on these individuals make it clear that most had been involved in corrupt dealings, although the report draws back from any *legal* findings of corruption.

Dawn is the hour when Akan Chiefs traditionally make their most solemn pronouncements; and it was at dawn on April 8, 1961, that Nkrumah went on the air to inform the people that he was going to cleanse the party and the government of corruption. Interpretations of the significance of the "Dawn Broadcast" vary widely. Geoffrey Bing, for example, argues that it signalled an honest attempt by Nkrumah to deal with corruption in his ministerial ranks to prepare the way for public acceptance of an austere budget;[42] Peter Omari asserts that what Nkrumah "really wanted was an opportunity to get rid of two of his comrades" so that he could "nullify any threat to his absolute control of the Party."[43] Whatever the true motivation for the announcement, no one denies that by the time it was made, many of Nkrumah's closest associates were overtly involved in corrupt dealings and had enriched themselves at party or government expense. Geoffrey Bing, Nkrumah's former attorney-general, discloses that a blue-ribbon commission investigated the assets of Nkrumah's ministers but its report was never published; the report was withheld mainly at the instance of Tawia Adamafio, one of the cabinet ministers who helped start the cleanup campaign in the first place. Also uncontested is the fact that the existence of extensive high-level corruption was so well known it had attracted wide public comment in Ghana—some of it, paradoxically, quite favorable[44]—and was even receiving unfavorable—and sometimes bemused—notice abroad.[45]

Admittedly, the overall picture that emerges from this review of the available evidence on Ghanaian political corruption up to 1966 is sketchy. It lacks detail on the internal workings of a broad range of central and local governmental units and agencies whose corrupt activities are only hinted in the auditors' reports and the reports proceeding from several pre-coup inquests. It definitely lacks both detail and firm outlines of the doings of Nkrumah and his close associates. Nevertheless, overall, the evidence to 1966 is sufficient to permit the conclusion that by that year acts of political corruption had become commonplace throughout the range of Ghanaian officialdom, from ministers of state down to lowly clerks in GNTC stores.

The Post-coup Revelations

On February 24, 1966, Ghana's Army and Police overthrew the regime of President Kwame Nkrumah. Two weeks later, on March 10, Lt.-Gen. J. A. Ankrah, then chairman of the junta's National Liberation Council (NLC), appointed a Commission of Inquiry headed by Justice Fred Apaloo to investigate the former president's assets; it was to be the first of more than forty commissions, committees, special audit teams, and other investigative bodies charged with probing the public and private activities of the Nkrumah regime (a list of these bodies may be found in Appendix A). There is little reason to doubt that the NLC had two principal, related reasons for setting these inquiries in motion: to discredit the Nkrumah regime as thoroughly as possible, and thereby to legitimize its seizure of power. There may also have been a third reason—to expose the depth and breadth of political corruption in Ghana with a view to doing something about it; at any rate, some military men five years after the NLC coup indicated this may have been the case.[46] Such late reflection admittedly rings of post-hoc rationalization,[47] but there can be little question that the military were genuinely preoccupied with the problem, and there are indications that even they were surprised at the richness of the catch pulled in by their legal fishermen. There is no way of knowing if most Ghanaians were surprised; somehow given the generally high level of Ghanaian political sophistication, it seems doubtful. That political corruption was pervasive at the upper levels of government was well known, and that it was common at the lower echelons could hardly have escaped notice in Ghana's face-to-face society. Again, what may have been lacking was knowledge of the details, and these were soon to be provided in numbing profusion.

It would only burden this study if we were to try to summarize the post-coup revelations in all their diversity. What can be done here, and what is more to the point, is to review some of those findings which relate to the question of whether Ghana had developed a culture of political corruption. Whatever else the Commissions of Inquiry did, they confirmed the general impression that political corruption had become commonplace all up and down the ranks of Ghanaian officialdom.

Nkrumah himself, despite the contrary objections of some of his champions[48] clearly was involved in a variety of corrupt transactions, particularly after a terrorist threw a hand grenade at him in the village of Kulungugu in January 1964. The assassination attempt may have unhinged him somewhat; W. Scott Thompson observes that not only did Ghana's foreign policy suffer thereafter, but "temptations which he had long held at bay could no longer be resisted. For a decade money had flowed about him, but it was always for the cause. . . . But now, 'the Ayeh-Kumi's of the world got to him, and to his deficiencies in character was added a new one, avarice.'"[49] There is some question about the actual extent of Nkrumah's personal fortune at the time of his divestiture.[50] There is no doubt, however, that he used public funds to distribute largesse to his favorites (he tapped the President's Contingency Vote* and at least two public corporation votes to buy cars for mistresses and to make various "gifts" to relatives, friends, associates, and ideological cronies). He also set up a special government agency, the National Development Corporation (NADECO, Ltd.), to facilitate the collection and handling of bribes, and the price paid by the government for properties purchased from a Greek businessman (A. G. Leventis) were deliberately inflated so that £ 1 million ($2,400,000) could be turned back to Nkrumah for his own use. At least £ 90,000 from the Leventis transaction went into Nkrumah's private bank account.[51] These are but highlights of dealings initiated by Nkrumah either personally or through his agents. The record also contains evidence of various valuable "gifts" he received, some under questionable circumstances. For example, one Henry K. Djaba, under prosecution for fraud allegedly committed in collaboration with officials in the Ministry of Agriculture and apparently hoping for a quashed indictment, presented Nkrumah with a £ 2,500 Mercedes-Benz sports car, a bulletproof Mercedes-Benz 600 worth £ 12,000, some £ 25,000 in cash allegedly intended for the CPP, and a £ 1,500 glider.[52] Nkrumah accepted the gifts, but Djaba was convicted and went to jail. It was suspected at the time that Nkrumah was worth considerably more than was uncovered by the Apaloo Commission, but all along investigators were hampered by difficulties in tracing the ex-President's assets. In any case, the evidence clearly shows that Nkrumah was personally involved in various corrupt acts.

The Apaloo Commission also outlined a theme that other commissions would fill out in fuller detail: it appeared that Nkrumah sat at the apex of a pyramid of government and party officials who had succeeded in institutionalizing political corruption at the highest levels, the Dawn Broadcast and all other exhortations to the contrary notwithstanding. Geoffrey Bing acknowledges that Nkrumah shied away from vigorous prosecution of his anti-corruption campaign, particularly following the Dawn Broadcast,[53] and even Sam Ikoku (a Nigerian Marxist adviser to Nkrumah) admits that many, if not most, of his own closest colleagues in government were implicated in corrupt and illegal transactions:

---

* "Votes" are approved and allocated funds or budgets.

In paragraph 69 of its Report, the Apaloo Commission estimated that the CPP's resources came from commissions of 5% to 10% on State transactions, on the one hand, and from contributions from Ghanaian and foreign corporations, on the other (cf. also para. 80). There is hardly any doubt that the collection of these funds was a means of personal enrichment for the high functionaries, the ministers, and the *permanents* (old-timers) of the party.[54]

At least five government bodies ostensibly set up for legitimate purposes turned out to be agencies for institutionalized political corruption: NADECO, the Ministry of Trade (in its import licensing role), the Guinea Press, the Ghana Bottling Company, and the National Papers Distribution Organization (NAPADO). All five organizations were objects of special NLC inquests.[55] The evidence of the Commissions of Inquiry indicates that the Guinea Press and NAPADO conducted their "legitimate" publication, distribution, and publicity activities largely for the benefit of the Party and governmental faithful and their clients. The Guinea Press was considered by Nkrumah to be his own property. He had put up the initial £ 20,000 for its incorporation (allegedly from CPP funds), he ran it through a dummy board of directors, and he directed its disposal in his first (1965) will, but there is no evidence he ever profited from it. Nevertheless, the Press received over £ 1.8 million from government sources and another £ 146,000 from the CPP. At the time of its dissolution it owed over N₵314,771. The investigating team that looked into the activities of the Press and its subsidiary, the Star Publishing Company, cited a high incidence of misappropriation, "dash," and extortion, and called the entire venture "a large cesspool of public waste."[56] Furthermore, they found that not the least of the functions of the Press was to provide "jobs for the boys," and that although it had a staff of 564 it had no personnel manager or rational employment policy. The report of the investigating team cites with approval a description in *The Ghanaian Times* of the Press's hiring practices:

"... the Guinea Press became something of an employment agency with incompetent and inefficient hands being pushed in on the Management by this Minister, the Chief, the Party official, just because that somebody, even through [*sic*] was a square peg in a round hole, was the nephew, niece, uncle, brother, son or relative of somebody. . . ." This assertion is amply proved by the evidence before us.[57]

NAPADO was the principal distributor of the publications of the Guinea Press—largely propaganda materials and government-owned newspapers. It, too, appears to have been a recipient of sizable amounts of public moneys for which there was little or no accounting; it, too, ran up large debts, which in this case were often assumed by other organizations at Nkrumah's orders. For all intents and purposes, the principal activity of NAPADO seems to have been to put money into the pockets of its chairman, W. Y. Eduful, and its board of directors, all persons nominated and controlled by Nkrumah.

As for the Ghana Bottling Company, it was set up with public funds but operated as a private firm, and its profits went to the CPP and Nkrumah.[58]

The abuses perpetrated by the Guinea Press, NAPADO, and the Ghana Bottling Company are small potatoes, however, when compared to those that were revealed in the National Development Company and the Ministry of Trade's import licensing operations. NADECO, according to Krobo Edusei, was the brainchild of Nkrumah, who said he had been told by an American friend that political parties in America were financed by companies. Nkrumah decided to create NADECO as receiver of the 5 to 10 percent commission he wanted levied on the price of all contracts negotiated by ministers, principal secretaries, and public corporations. Edusei's candid summary of its purpose bears quoting: "When many bribes started flowing in, NADECO was formed for all the bribes to be channeled into."[59]

To be sure, NADECO conducted some legitimate insurance business as well, but even in this sphere its operations were tainted. Not only were government employees forced to insure their automobiles through NADECO, but foreign insurance companies with Ghanaian clients were required to use NADECO as their agent and, naturally, to pay well for the privilege. In any case, the company's principal sources of funds were bribes, "commissions," and "gifts" that were either freely given or extorted from a wide variety of European companies operating in Ghana as well as from a number of Ghanaian building contractors. Among the firms contributing to NADECO's coffers were ZIM Navigation, an Israeli firm that had contracted to operate Ghana's merchant marine; Parkinson-Howard, a large British pharmaceutical firm; Henschel, a German truck manufacturer; and Duncan Gilbey and Matheson, the British firm that makes, among other products, Gilbey's gin. Withal, the Azu Crabbe Commission found that by the time of the coup NADECO had received a total of £ 1,697,000 from a variety of sources. Of that amount, some £ 90,000 went into Nkrumah's private bank account, another £ 215,000 went to the CPP Appeal Fund, and various other sums were disbursed loans to Nkrumah's pet enterprises (for example, £ 5,187 to the Ghana Bottling Company and as gifts—disguised as loans—to several of Nkrumah's girl friends. Still other sums were simply directed by Nkrumah to private uses (as, for example, to construct houses for his former cook and three of his relatives.)

As was indicated earlier, the grant of import licenses was the object of two Commissions of Inquiry during the Nkrumah regime, one in 1964 and the other in 1965. Whereas pre-coup probers had found it difficult to get hard evidence of corrupt transactions, however, the post-coup Ollenu Commission encountered no such difficulty. The Ollenu investigation found not only that high-level officials (including former trade ministers A. Y. K. Djin and Kwesi Armah) were involved in corrupt deals with import licenses, but that the problem was greatly extended and structured:

> ... the attendant bribery and corruption were ... not spasmodic but organized and systematically operated through agents at different levels of society, and involving various persons, some of them supposedly respectable and obviously unsuspected. So well organized was this business that, against their will, decent importers were compelled to accept the improper methods of obtaining licenses as the only means of survival.[60]

The commission lists some 52 separate corrupt transactions involving licenses whose total worth was over £ 5,000,000; of this number, 17 are described in specific details, and these 17 account for some £ 2,958,600 worth of licenses which brought in almost £ 120,000 in illegal commissions and bribes. The remaining £ 2 million worth of licenses were procured under what the commission characterized as fraudulent, extortionary, or otherwise illegal circumstances.[61] The report also reveals the uncomplicated manner in which most corrupt transactions were made. A good example is to be found in the case of Kwesi Armah, the former Ghana High Commissioner in London who held the post of minister of foreign trade from July 1965 until the coup. The foreign trade minister was charged with reviewing all applications for import licenses to decide whether a commission should be levied as a condition for approval, and if so, what percentage of a license's value should be assessed. Armah practiced what the investigating commission called "selectivity" in his decisions: government agencies usually were not charged; Armah's close friends and clients often got licenses for greater value than they requested and in exchange paid either a 5 percent commission or no commission at all, and everybody else paid between 5 percent and 10 percent directly to the minister or his agents.[62] What happened to the "commissions" that were collected? Evidence on this point is sparse. According to at least one former high oficial who was interviewed during 1970–71, proceeds were normally distributed according to the number of intermediaries or agents involved, and in consideration of whether Nkrumah knew of the transaction and demanded a share for himself or one of his other agencies, whether a contribution to the CPP was required, and so forth. (See Chapter 4 for one official's estimated breakdown of his own expenditures.) The author was given to understand by several Ghanaian informants that NADECO was one frequent beneficiary of corrupt transactions involving import licenses.

The four agencies discussed above, of course, represent merely a part of the visible tip of the iceberg of political corruption during the Nkrumah regime. The evidence indicates that they were the most highly institutionalized agencies for political corruption, to be sure (and our summary hardly does justice to the extent and ramification of the activities in which their directors, agents, officials, patrons, and numerous clients were involved); but the post-coup inquests produced ample evidence of political corruption in various other governmental and quasi-governmental agencies and corporations, in municipal and urban councils, and in the country's three universities. Among the other units that received special scrutiny were the United Ghana Farmers' Co-operative Council, the Cocoa Marketing Board, the Football Pools Authority, the Workers' Brigade, the Central Organization of Sports, the Ghana Cargo Handling Company, the Ghana Timber Marketing Board, the Ghana Timber Co-operative Union, the State Furniture and Joinery Corporation, the First Ghana Building Society, the Ghana Trades Union Congress, the State Distilleries Corporation, the State Housing Corporation, the Ghana Prisons, the State Publishing Corporation, and the Ashanti Goldfields Corporation. Still other probes and special audits, for which reports have yet to be published, investigated the State Fisheries Corporation, the CPP organization, the Young Pioneers, the Ghana Muslim Council, the Ideological Institute at Winneba, the African Affairs Centre, the Bureau of African Affairs, the National Council of Ghana Women, the Young Farmers' League, the State Tobacco Products Corporation, and the Black Star Line. In all, some forty-two governmental or semi-governmental units were investigated; in addition, the auditor-general's report for 1965–66 (filed in 1968) reveals evidence of corrupt dealings and practices in a large number of other government units that never came under special investigation.

Characteristically, all the state enterprises and agencies in which corruption flourished seemed to share what the Auditor-General's Office characterized as "certain weaknesses ... namely, lack of adequate capital, poor management, political interference and shortage of spare parts and raw materials."[63] Further, "Another striking feature of the operations of the Corporations was the vast extent of the indebtedness with one another,"[64] which gives evidence of their general unwillingness to calculate and bear responsibility for the costs of their activities.* The State Farms Corporation, by all accounts one of the most corruption-ridden of the state agencies, managed by the end of 1965 to accumulate an unusually large net deficit: ₵17,248,784. The auditor-general's appraisal of the causes of that deficit reads much like the explanations made about other agencies:

> Political decisions such as the large-scale transfer of labour to the Corporation in 1964 on the dissolution of the Cocoa Division, deficit on the revaluation of assets, lack of labour control, unproductive projects undertaken, bulk purchases of unsuitable vehicles and plant and machinery, poor management, inadequate control over expenditure and inefficient accounting system were among the other factors which contributed to this colossal loss. . . . Many defalcations and losses occurred.[65]

---

* This characteristic, of course, is not peculiar to Ghanaian corporations but is generally shared by state corporations. A case in point is the British Overseas Food Corporation, which administered the disastrous Tanganyika groundnuts scheme after 1946. For details, see Alan Wood, *The Groundnut Affair* (London: The Bodley Head, 1950).

The NLC and Busia Periods, 1966–69, 1969–72

Among the explanations the National Liberation Council offered to justify its seizure of power in February 1966 was that the Nkrumah regime was so hopelessly corrupt it must be displaced before the system as a whole could be cleansed.[66] It was to confirm this contention that the new regime immediately launched its series of probes and Commissions of Inquiry, and ultimately these investigations produced enough evidence to convince most Ghanaians that the NLC's charge of widespread corruption was true. (Whether the revelations also succeeded in justifying the military's intervention in the eyes of most Ghanaians is, of course, another question, but it lies beyond the scope of this analysis.) Broadly implicit in the NLC argument was the further conclusion that Ghana's new military rulers were morally justified in their actions because they were not themselves corrupt.

The available evidence suggests that indeed the military's record was relatively clean. There had been allegations at the court martial of Capt. Benjamin Awaithey in 1958 that a number of military men were involved in corrupt dealings, but all those allegations were made to support a charge of conspiracy against the regime.[67] There were also some charges made by Nkrumah after his deposition that the U.S. Central Intelligence Agency and/or the American Embassy in Accra gave the coup leaders large sums of money to do their deed,[68] but these charges were never substantiated. In sum, apart from the Awaithey matter there is no public record of military men involved in anything more than a few instances of petty corruption before the coup. The military's image as the champion of public morality suffered one rather sharp setback after the coup when in April 1969 it was revealed that no less a person than the chairman of the NLC, Gen. Joseph Ankrah, had wittingly sanctioned a covert collection of moneys on behalf of his own possible candidature for the country's presidency.[69] On that occasion an embarrassed NLC forced Ankrah to resign, and he was replaced by Brig. Gen. A. A. Afrifa. Otherwise, the NLC completed its term in office without major scandal. In 1969 the NLC gracefully ceded power to a popularly elected government headed by Dr. Kofi A. Busia, a former Professor of Sociology at the University of Ghana. The Busia regime was unable to come to terms with the country's many economic and political problems and was in turn deposed by the military on January 14, 1972.

Not unexpectedly, the military junta that overthrew the government of Dr. Busia also immediately launched investigations into the assets of its predecessors. At the time of this writing, the two new commissions appointed by the junta had not yet reported, and the one continued from before the coup (the Anin Corruption Inquiry) had issued only three interim reports. There were indications that there was some political corruption among members of the Busia government, but apparently on a much smaller scale than was attained during the Nkrumah regime.

Busia himself refused to testify before the Taylor Assets Committee and thereby fell under the committee's operating presumption that his assets were illegally acquired unless proven otherwise. He may in fact have been worth a good deal before he assumed office in 1969 (he then had assets over $800,000, according to his own declaration,[70]) but even so it appeared that he would have a good deal to explain. For example, questions had arisen over the matter of the house built for him in his home town, Wenchi, while he was in office; he maintained it cost $155,000, but there were indications it may actually have cost as much as $300,000.[71] Investigators were also interested to know the source of the approximately $74,000 in cash he brought into the country in a trunk when he returned to Ghana in 1966.[72] The $12,000 collected by a friend for the former minister of the interior, Chief Simon Dombo, was another subject of speculation,[73] as were three deposits totaling $99,000 made in three months to the private account of G. D. Ampaw, former minister of health,[74] and the string of company directorships and businesses acquired by B. J. Da Rocha after he became the Progress Party's general secretary.[75]

If documented evidence of political corruption at the upper governmental levels during the 1966–72 period was inconclusive or still indefinite, the auditor-general's reports for the 1967–69 period revealed that not much had changed since Nkrumah's days at the local levels of government and in the statutory bodies. Of the 142 separate local government units operating in the country in that two-year period, 102 reported on their accounts for 1967–68, and 90 for 1968–69. During those two years, 65 percent of the units reporting showed losses; those losses totaled $465,586, of which perhaps 90 percent was attributable to various acts of embezzlement, misappropriation, stealing, etc., by officials.[76] By American standards this figure might seem rather modest. By Ghanaian standards it is quite high, since it represents, by extrapolation, between 15 and 25 percent of most local units' budgets. Of the local officials displaying the greatest mendacity, tax and revenue collectors led all the rest, followed by treasurers and secretary-treasurers of local councils. The 100 public boards and state corporations during 1967–69 suffered losses amounting to $37,187,406, of which perhaps 50 to 60 percent (by the kindest interpretation of the facts in the auditor's report) could be laid to various illegal or corrupt acts. Twenty-eight of the public bodies suffered net operating losses, and in thirty-six, there was evidence of fraud, misappropriation, and the like. Almost without exception, the heaviest losses were in those public bodies with commercial or quasi-commercial operations.[77]

It is interesting to observe that the combined 1967–69 losses for all reporting public bodies, including educational institutions and local governments, totaled $37,937,733, and that this figure is roughly 5 percent of the aggregate budget expenditures for the national government during the same two-year period (that is, roughly 5 percent of $752,978,984; the nearly $38-million figure is *not* included in the two-year national budget deficit of $161,555,512[78]). Given such figures, it is tempting to infer that a cash value might be assigned for political corruption in Ghana. However, if Ghana in fact contained anything like an incipient culture of political corruption in 1970, the costs of corruption at all levels from the highest governmental precincts to the lowest would be literally incalculable. For one thing, many of the activities it embraced would be conducted beyond the pale of public scrutiny and would not be reflected in any report. For another, much of it inevitably would have involved trading in intangible political goods, which can be assigned dollar value only in certain discrete instances and usually cannot be assessed in the aggregate at any level of officialdom. (This aspect of assessing corruption is discussed in greater detail in chapter 4.)

Can we nevertheless establish the existence of a culture of political corruption in Ghana on the basis of the data cited thus far? It appears that the documentary evidence on the extent, operation, and growth of political corruption permits the conclusion that at least on the level of visible official behavior, a case has been established for the existence of an incipient Ghanaian culture of political corruption. What is perhaps lacking is detail on the incidence of political corruption at the lowest levels of officialdom. For that, we turn briefly to personal observation.

During my two-year stay in Ghana, I made eight round trips between Accra and Lome, the Togo capital, which lies on the seacoast just over the Ghana-Togo border. On each trip, I faced customs inspection on both sides of the frontier, and in addition, on each return trip to Accra I was stopped two or more times by Ghana police roadblocks. The ostensible purpose of the roadblocks was to catch smugglers bringing dutiable goods from Togo. On every trip but one, I was asked by one or more of the police or customs officials I encountered for "gifts," "dash," or "favour," either to "prevent" a levy of customs or simply to be allowed to proceed without further trouble. Every one of my friends and acquaintances who had made the same trip related similar experiences, but with one distinction: Ghanaians, particularly those of low status, tended to be subjected to greater harassment than expatriates, possibly because expatriates or influential Ghanaians were more likely to register formal protest. Every so often one read that a policeman or a customs officer had been convicted of extorting money (usually in exchange for a promise that a violator of the law would not be prosecuted), but most such instances were never even reported.[79]

In 1970, the inspector general of police, B. A. Yakubu, apparently felt it necessary to warn his officers that continued bribe-taking, extortion, and other corrupt practices would be dealt with harshly; and in 1971 the government instituted a policy of frequent rotation of officers assigned to customs and border patrol duties, principally to prevent them from cultivating "clients" who would pay them smuggling bribes on a regular basis.

Again, it may be necessary to point out that not all Ghanaian policemen were corrupt; probably most of them were not. But corruption was sufficiently widespread within their ranks to foster a common opinion that Ghanaian policemen were on the take. It is fair to say that officials in other areas of public service were similarly regarded. This view was reflected in the constant exhortations, warnings, and homilies about corruption offered by educators, political and social leaders, and journalists,[80] and no doubt it was reinforced by the frequent newspaper revelations of a seemingly endless variety of corrupt activities by officials throughout the country. To cite but a few examples, the press in 1970–71 reported sales of passport forms and job application forms, "surcharges" on import permits, "fees" paid to firemen for putting out fires, "tips" for the use of "closed" public roads, imported goods stolen and resold before they cleared customs, "tips" charged to expedite paperwork (even for fellow bureaucrats), misappropriation of local council funds by clerks and treasurers, and use of official vehicles as taxis or for private transport.[81] An extraordinarily petty kind of misappropriation occurred frequently in post offices: the resale of used but uncancelled postage stamps.[82]

In sum; the Ghanaian consensus concerning public officials in the early 1970s was well described by a noted Ghanaian educator:

He [Dr. J. Yanney-Ewusie] described the public image of the public service as "an institution in which one can work as little as one liked for as much money as one's trade union can get for him." Others, Dr. Yanney-Ewusie said, regarded the public service as a place for creating fringe benefits through pilfering, bribes, and the misuse of public property...." The typical public servant, Dr. Ewusie said, "is visualized as the man wearing a tie and an important look on his face who knows how to complicate simplicity."[83]

3

The Culture of Political Corruption:
Supportive Values

One element of any political culture is the structure of supportive values and orientations that define, among other things, what is politically legitimate in society and what is not. In Ghana, the development of an incipient culture of political corruption was accompanied by an evolving structure of values that had the effect of rationalizing, if not legitimizing, corrupt behavior. Between December 1970 and June 1971, the author had the opportunity to interview in depth a dozen men who were actively involved in the widespread corruption of the Nkrumah regime, and to explore at length the values and attitudes that underlay their behavior. The interviewees are not identified in this study since all were promised absolute anonymity, but it can be reported that all were officials either in the Nkrumah government or in the Convention People's Party. One was a junior minister, two held high party office, and the rest operated at various official and semi-official levels of the regime. By the time they were interviewed, most of them had gone into business and several were dealing regularly with the current government. Only two were technically unemployed, but even these admitted they had stable sources of income, in both cases deriving in part from investments and contacts made during their terms in office.

The author explored the twelve respondents' political values in four main areas: (1) general attitudes toward authority, authority figures, and government; (2) perceptions of political efficacy; (3) parameters of obligation and individual responsibility; and (4) retrospective attitudes concerning their own corrupt behavior and the like behavior of others. It must be emphasized that the interviews were conducted informally, although the respondents were told in advance what predetermined themes were being explored. Thus, expressions of political values often emerged in discussions of other matters, and of course not always in the sequence in which the four themes are noted above. A few quotations from the interviews illustrate some representative patterns within each area.

General Attitudes toward Authority

The only man who ever could tell me what to do, and who I respected, was my father and sometimes my uncle K_____. The chief, he was a big thiefman. My father listened to him, but I only did because I had to. . . . Nkrumah too was thiefman; he said big things, but everyone knew he liked pretty woman too much, posh cars and money. (Mr. *D*; Interview D-6)

Government always promise more than it gives; only if the smart men get together can we get what we need. (Mr. *K*, Interview K-2)

R (Respondent): Any man who believes what the chief or the DC [District Commissioner] or a minister tells him is a fool. Sometimes you have to do what they tell you or be put in jail; but if you go to jail, you are not very wise.
I (Interviewer): But do you obey only if you are afraid of going to jail?
R: Sometimes. But most you obey if it is better to obey than to disobey. But it is better to avoid having to make the choice whether to obey or not obey. (Mr. *B*; Interview B-5)

All government is bad. English, Nkrumah, NLC, Busia—all cannot be trusted, at all, at all!* I do well under English [and] Nkrumah, because I know that only if you are a big man you can get what you want. This is the Ghanaian way. (Mr. *G*; Interview G-6)

These comments reflect, if nothing else, a high degree of generalized political cynicism, as well as a sharp awareness of the personal, instrumental aspects of politics. There is no hard evidence

_____
* "At all!" is a Ghanaian colloquialism signifying an emphatic negative, as in the following exchange: "Is *X* an honest man?" "At all!"

that all or most Ghanaians shared these views of politics and authority, but certain qualified observers, such as Maxwell Owusu (whose views are cited later in this chapter), suggest that these attitudes are far more prevalent than hitherto suspected. Certainly the comments cited accurately represent the views and values of the twelve interviewees concerned in the immediate analysis, and if these men are at all representative of those involved in politically corrupt dealings in Ghana—as we suspect they are—it is reasonable to infer that their views reflect those of the larger group.

Perceptions of Political Efficacy and Competence

As the term is generally used in political science, "political efficacy" refers to an individual's ability to influence political outcomes. It implies, for most purposes, the individual's concept of his own "political competence," that is, his perception of the extent to which he can effect political outcomes favorable to himself or to those with whom he identifies.[1]

The twelve respondents all professed to understand what made the Ghanaian polity work. Each in his own terms named the key levers of authority and influence as he saw them, and each could describe at length the means by which he obtained what he wanted from the system. Not unexpectedly, the levers named and the methods described tended to be those of indirection, usually operating through informal rather than formal channels.

It was not that the respondents were unaware of formal structures and channels, or of the norms that circumscribed the conduct of official business: indeed, most of them could still, after four or five years out of office, cite chapter and verse of the regulations that governed their positions. Rather, they tended to pursue these regular channels in conducting what one called "ordinary business"—that is, for transactions in which they had little personal interest, or which involved matters of routine. However, once their self-interest was engaged or some important social or political obligation was involved, they preferred to operate through informal channels and by informal methods. Finally, in light of such attitudes and behavior it is hardly surprising that the respondents all claimed to know the "right" people, that is, those who could be relied upon to do their bidding or advance their cause, or with whom mutually profitable exchanges could be initiated and maintained. On any scale of perceived political efficacy, then, the twelve respondents would rank very high indeed. A few of their comments highlight these observations:

> I: If you wished, for example, Government to accept your tender or a contract rather than someone else's, how should you—or anybody else—go about it?
> R: I could always, or almost always, get my friends' tenders considered first. Now they do not heed me because they are afraid of Busia. Some day it will be changed again. But any smart man who has friends or family in the right place can get what he wants—if you do not forget to "dash" [bribe, or gift] proper. (Mr. *C*; Interview C-7)

> Ask and you shall receive. But do not ask too much, or too big man. But even a small, small man can get a favor from a big man if his gift is right, or if his uncle asks for him. . . . We say, "mouth smile, but money smile better." (Mr. *K*; Interview K-4)

> It is all a matter of knowing where to go and whom to see. Once you learn the men in power, who their friends are, and their family, there are always ways to receive favorable treatment. . . . I never had any difficulty securing my way once I had learned my lessons. (Mr. *E*; Interview E-5)

> You know Ghana saying, "Monkey de work, baboon de chop." [The wise man profits from the fool's labors.] I am always baboon! (Mr. *D*; Interview D-3)

Parameters of Obligation and Responsibility

In the absence of reliable hierarchies of trust, political and social intercourse becomes impossible. Both social structures and political structures function partly to provide precisely such hierarchies of trust, the one through bonds of natural or simulated consanguinity, the other through symbols and institutions that seek to replicate the ties of the social structure and bind men to common tasks and objectives. Such structures in varying degrees make it possible to predict human affairs; the looser or weaker the structures, the less predictable the social and political outcomes, and the tighter or stronger, the more predictable. Despite evidence that primary group loyalties have undergone serious erosion in modern industrialized societies, the primary group remains the prime focus of trust in most developing nations. The family, the clan, the village, even the ethnic group, encompasses those people who are most apt to be trustworthy, or at least those with whom social intercourse is likely to be possible with minimal friction. Correspondingly, certain obligations—of reciprocal trust, loyalty, service, and perhaps obedience—are embedded in each circle of affiliation, becoming specific or generalized according to the expectations of the group.

It has been widely asserted that the "modern men" of Ghana, because of their involvement in political groups and institutions beyond the primary group, have adjusted their hierarchies of trust to accommodate their broader involvements. At the very least, it is claimed, those operating within governmental institutions have experienced the sorts of conflicts of role and loyalty that afflicted Lloyd Faller's Busoga "Bantu bureaucrats."[2] These assertions may be generally accurate; there is scant empirical evidence on the subject, and Faller's study has not been replicated in Ghana. But if they are accurate, then the dozen men interviewed for this study, all admittedly "modern men" in the sense that their political and economic behavior suggests strongly held instrumental or secular values, somehow depart from the legal norm in terms of their loyalties, and hence their perceived obligations. Their observations indicate that broadened loyalties did not necessarily attend their involvement in the national political arena.

> I see first my mother, my uncles, my father, my brothers,* my countryman** and I help them first. I know them, but do I know Ghana government, or Ghana court? (Mr. *H*; Interview H-2)

---

* In Ghanaian colloquial usage, "brother" is used to refer not only to a blood brother but to any male member of the extended family except one's father or uncles, and often even to any male from one's own village or area. In any event, "brother" indicates membership in some sort of primary group. "Sister" is often used in the same way.

** The colloquial "countryman," (or "countrywoman") may refer to someone from the same village or the same area as the speaker, or

The politicians, the ministers, the MPs, even the civil servants with their regulations said much at first about working for Ghana's good. We were all proud to bring Ghana to democracy and to do better than the English, who only wanted to exploit us. Nkrumah said so, and we believed him. Then everybody started to chop*** money, chop cars, chop stores, and those who didn't chop and said it was unlawful were soon sacked. So I learned my lessons and chopped without worry, for myself and my brothers. (Mr. *J*; Interview J-7)

I: But don't the regulations forbid trading in official favors? And if a civil servant does that, don't his acts hurt the country?
R: No. If government doesn't help the people, then civil servants are right in helping them. And if I am posted to K_____, I help my family and countrymen first, because they know me and would be angry if I did not. (Mr. *C*; Interview C-4)

Retrospective Attitudes

The A_____ Commission of Enquiry found I had exceeded my income by £ _____, and I had to pay that. But I am not sorry; I used the money wisely. (Mr. *G*; Interview G-3)

When Busia is gone, I will be back in Service. And unless the soldiers stand by my desk, I will do what I did before, because no one can stay in office unless he prefers those who serve him well. (Mr. *A*; Interview A-5)

Do you want me to feel guilty about what happened? Guilt is for pastors and priests. If I give drink gift to the chief, a gift to a big man is also the Ghana way. (Mr. *K*; Interview K-4)

---

it may simply refer to someone from the same ethnic group. In any case, it usually implies co-ethnicity except when used by Ghanaians abroad, when it may simply refer to another Ghanaian.

*** "Chop" or "chap" is a widely used west African pidgin word meaning generally "to eat," or simply "food." Ghanaian colloquial usage gives it the additional meaning "to take," or more crassly "to steal." "Chop" is also used to mean "strike down" or "hit," as in the phrase, "A de chop um good," which means "I hit him hard."

The above quotations represent but a small sampling of the retrospective attitudes expressed by the twelve respondents. Nevertheless, they incorporate the general themes and values common to all their conversations in the same vein.

All respondents admitted violating the formal norms; moreover all suggested that rules against corruption apply only to the losers in the zero-sum game of Ghanaian politics, while those on top, the winners, can conveniently disregard them.[3] Everyone flouts the rules, they said; anyone who might insist on their literal application could not survive politically.[4]

Most of the respondents saw their current out-of-power, out-of-office situation as temporary, a result of political bad luck which the future could well reverse to their renewed profit.

The respondents were on the whole a thoroughly unrepentant lot, contemptuous of the Busia regime in particular and of government in general. So far from exhibiting guilt or remorse over their alleged misdeeds, they argued that they had acted as they did out of necessity, in order to reduce the uncertainty of what they perceived to be a sort of Hobbesian world in which every man's hand, if not set against his neighbor, was at least groping in his pocket.

All respondents articulated extremely high levels of political cynicism, ascribing self-seeking motives not only to most of their colleagues during the Nkrumah era, but to officials in the Busia regime as well. It was only with respect to the military, who ousted them, that they exhibited any ambivalence; four conceded that most of the members of the (military) National Liberation Council were honest and uncorrupted, although three others pointedly recalled the resignation of NLC Chairman Gen. Ankrah (for privately collecting of money to finance his presidential aspirations) as proof that "moral" soldiers are not immune to corruption.

The respondents could be adjudged as perfect a set of economic men as any that economists postulate in theory. They appeared to be wholly rational in their actions, wholly calculating, and genuinely convinced that their admittedly illicit behavior was justified by reason of their loyalties to kin, friends, clients, and ethnic brethren. What is more, they apparently were prepared to do it all again if given the chance.

They also displayed a sense of political efficacy that was unexpectedly positive in light of their current situations. Not only did they profess to a thorough knowledge of how to get around the system; they were wholly convinced that given the proper settings and opportunities, they could once again manipulate men and events to their own ends. This attitude would not have been so startling had it been expressed by only a few of the respondents; in that case one might feel tempted to dismiss it as wishful thinking. But every single one of this forceful, generally realistic group appeared to share the feeling, and thus it is difficult not to give some credence to their claim.

Finally, the twelve respondents were wholly parochial political men whose politics seemed invariably circumscribed by the range of their pragmatic interests. They showed no reluctance to identify themselves as Ghanaians, to be sure, but for most it appeared that this identity implied little of operational consequence. A generalized ordering of their socio-political hierarchy of identification—and hence of their hierarchy of trust—could be set out as follows (in order of importance):

1. Nuclear family and/or extended family
2. Close friends/"countrymen"/co-ethnics
3. Business associates
4. "Old boys" (school classmates)
5. Clients/supporters (usually persons in categories 1, 2, 4)
6. Professional/official colleagues
7. Persons in superior/superordinate official and social positions
8. The country (the government and/or its institutions)

The categories set out above need some explanation, as does their ranking. First, the categories are not mutually exclusive. It is likely, for example, that all of those in category 1 (kinsmen) could also be included in category 2 (co-ethnics and close friends), that some of those in categories 1 and 2 would be included in category 5 (clients and supporters), and so on. The categories and their ranking emerged in part from sets of questions designed to probe three dimensions of trust and identification: (a) the persons to whom a respondent would turn when in difficulty, (b) the persons or institutions with whom a respondent preferred to deal in most official and social matters, and (c) the persons, groups, or institutions to whom a respondent felt he owed obligations and loyalties. The categories and the order in which they are ranked constitute a generalized sum of the respondents' answers and to those that dealt with more general attitudes to authority, obligation, and the like. Each category, therefore, represents a collective statement concerning relative *levels* of trust and identification. Thus, category 3 could be read as follows: "Business associates tend to be trusted more than 'old boys,' clients and supporters, official colleagues, or persons in superior positions, unless any of the latter happen to be co-ethnics or kinsmen."

Second, the categories assume that trust implies identification, and vice versa, because in practice, the persons, groups, and institutions with whom one most closely identifies, are also those most likely to be objects of considerable trust. In our set of categories, number 6 (the country) is the only depersonalized object listed; it is ranked last precisely because the respondents saw institutions of government as objects of last resort. Political and social relations in Ghana tend to be personalized in the extreme, and when Ghanaians think of transactions within or with the formal polity, they do so in terms of relations with individuals or discrete groups of individuals rather than with institutions. Trust is given to specific persons or groups with familiar, non-threatening attributes. Institutions rank lowest on the scale of trust and identification because their impersonal nature makes them—in the Ghanaian situation—both unpredictable and arbitrary.

A final note on the interviews. The author concedes that the respondents did not in any sense constitute a statistically valid sample of the corrupt officials of the Nkrumah regime. (Indeed, there appears to be no way to estimate that population reliably; respondents' estimates, for example, ranged all the way from twenty to seventy-five percent of *all* Ghanaian office-holders.) Conceivably, then, what is generalized above from twelve sets of interviews may be largely unrepresentative of the values held by most of those involved in corrupt practices. Moreover, by any criterion of selection the twelve respondents were members of Ghana's former political elite, and it is possible that bureaucrats and functionaries who served at the lower levels of government and the party might hold generally different values. But analyses by other observers, Ghanaians and non-Ghanaians alike, indicate that our respondents were indeed representative in their attitudes, representative not only of the larger population of persons involved in politically corrupt dealings, but in some degree of most politically aware Ghanaians. For example, Margaret Field, whose classic ethno-psychiatric study of rural Ghana remains one of the most insightful analyses of the Ghanaian psyche, notes that one of the prime characteristics of the Akan social and political structure (i.e., of southern and central Ghana) is "the absence of hide-bound rigidity." This condition, Field asserts, proceeds from the following attitudes and values:

> Class hardly exists; rank does exist but its attainment is the reward of individual merit. Institutions were made for man. Nothing is immune from criticism. Justice is more than law. The spirit of the law is more than the letter.[5]

"Of course," she notes, "this adaptability and flexibility cut both ways: the self-seeking opportunist has no hampering scruples."[6]

The last word on the value structure that supports the political culture of Ghana belongs properly to a Ghanaian. We have noted how our respondents conveyed the image of nearly perfect economic men, how they depicted the system as a sort of Hobbesian jungle in which illicit behavior was justified in the interests of political self-preservation and fulfillment of obligations to kinship or to other primary ties. Maxwell Owusu, in his excellent study of local politics in Agona-Swedru (again, south-central Ghana), persuasively argues a view of Ghanaian politics in which

> The exercise of power, chiefly, colonial, and party, was seen as a major means of achieving, protecting, and advancing individual, family, and status-class or group economic and other material advantages and interests. The struggle for power . . . was primarily a struggle in relation to the possession of wealth and its distribution and consumption to achieve high social status, prestige, and social privilege.[7]

Thus, "Changes in power relations tend[ed] to reflect, to a very large extent, changes in the control, distribution, and generalized consumption of wealth."[8]

> What is often forgotten or not realized [Owusu points out], is that the political development in Ghana, particularly between 1950 and 1966 . . . was characterized by a political process in which individuals and groups in various local areas supported and voted for this or that group or political party in terms largely of instrumental values expressed by

individual opportunism and careerism.... Other techniques in the
political process were "crossing the carpet," bribery, corruption.....[9]

Owusu does not, it should be noted, advance an analysis based on a
Ghanaian variety of economic determinism; rather, he asserts there
has been an "economization" of political relations, so that political
transactions are colored and often dominated by economic interest.
From his perspective, what we have here called "political corruption"
is seen as but one of a large variety of self-serving political modes that
are instrumental in determining the important questions of who rules,
what political resources are distributed or consumed, and who will
benefit from the exercise of public authority. If Owusu is correct, the
values expressed by the twelve respondents may be even more
generally held than the interviewees themselves suggested. And if that
is indeed the case, the source of support for a Ghanaian culture of
political corruption seems obvious.

The cut-off date for Owusu's discussion of Swedru and Ghana is
1966, and it might be argued that his comments therefore do not apply
to the post-coup period. The author's own first-hand observations,
however, indicated that Owusu's propositions were equally applicable
during the Busia period; the same conclusion seems to have been
reached by three Progress Party MPs during parliamentary debates in
1970 and 1971:

> Mr. E. K. Addae (PP—Ashanti–Akim North):... During the old regime
> there were reports of embezzlement of state funds, laziness on the part
> of some public employees, malingering and sorts of dubious deeds
> leading to the loss of public funds. All these evils are prevalent in our
> society today and they have to be eradicated; else the progress we talk
> so much about today will never come to pass.[10]

> Mr. George Oteng (PP—Asiakwa–Kwaben):... The idea of everybody
> in Ghana trying to get rich quick, building a house at the expense of
> others, especially of the Government, is what is ruining the country.
> This idea inherited by Ghanaians is taking firm root.[11]

> Mr. M. Archer (PP—Wasa East):... Any time I stand up and say that
> people are corrupt, Members in this House think I am joking. I am not
> joking at all. I say that with all seriousness. What we saw and what we

listened to during the deliberations of the Public Accounts Committee is evidence of the fact that people in this country—in fact many of them—are corrupt. . . . One thing that I should like to say is that many people in this country think that it is only politicians who are corrupt. . . . But those who are most corrupt are civil servants and people in the public corporations. . . . Only Heaven knows how much we are losing in this country through the practice of corruption.[12]

– 4 –

The Anatomy of Corruption:
The Process at Three Levels

One of the basic assumptions of this study is that the office-holder in the formal polity occupies a pivotal position in the process of political corruption because he is the one who determines whether or not the political goods available to him will be dispensed in politically corrupt transactions. Most transactions which manifestly violate written or unwritten norms of official behavior can be readily characterized as "corrupt" within the terms of our definition, The distinction between corrupt transactions and non-corrupt transactions loses much of its clarity, however, when we consider transactions that are technically illicit or extra-legal yet sanctioned by usage or convention. In some societies, bureaucratic short-cutting, informal brokerage, and payment of "normal" or "expected" rewards for services rendered by office-holders become so much a part of standard operating procedure that they acquire their own semi-legality. In the Soviet Union, for example, the *tolkach* (expediter) remains very much a part of contemporary society because he offers services that may be essential when managers choose to operate indirectly to attain ends thwarted by bureaucratic blockage or some other systemic failure.[1] Yet, as Steven Staats points out, "Such widespread informal mechanisms are not sanctioned by the rules or ideology of the system—i.e., they are corrupt."[2]

In Africa, the function of the political broker is usually not as precisely defined as that of the Soviet *tolkach*, but comparable services are performed in various contexts and by various agents and intermediaries, both inside and outside the formal polity. In Ghana, for example, what could be called an "advance man" prepares the way for ministerial bush tours and subsequently expedites transactions;[3] similarly, "verandah boys" have commonly performed expediting tasks for their patrons.[4] Such persons seem to gravitate naturally to corrupt milieux, and just as naturally to become part of the networks of transactional relationships that tend to engraft themselves upon basic corruption dyads. However, it is difficult to identify the expediter, much less to specify the services he performs, the scope of his operations, and his methods of procuring results, in a generalized discussion. What is needed is a case-history analysis that provides such detail as is necessary to clarify the roles of principals, agents, brokers, and other participants in both the core-process and the extended-process aspects of political corruption. This chapter examines the case of ex-Ministerial Secretary *A* as the central figure in one network of corrupt relationships, and from this case history draws some inferences about the corruption of Ghanaian officials in general. It also examines the case of the Football Pools Authority, which illustrates political corruption in an institutional setting. And finally, it seeks to discover the possible outlines of an informal polity in Ghana.

The Case of Mr. A

[In the following discussion certain details that might permit identification of Mr. *A* have been either changed or deleted, but the account remains much as it was told to the author. Quotations are direct, with the permission of Mr. *A*.][5]

At the time of the interviews, Mr. *A* was in his mid-forties, married, the father of several children. He was born in a "relatively prosperous" town in southeast Ghana, to parents who enjoyed some affluence thanks to the trading activities of the larger family. *A* graduated from one of the better private secondary schools in Ghana and acquired a B.A. degree in economics through the University of London's external examinations scheme. Immediately following the award of his university degree, he was appointed to the Gold Coast civil service, where, by virtue of his talents, he won rapid promotion. He was drawn to the CPP in 1957 and became active in the party despite official constraints on civil servants' political activities. By 1962 he had acquired what he described as a "local leadership" role in the unofficial civil servants' activist group of the CPP. In 1963 his combined skills as party activist and senior civil servant were recognized by the Nkrumah government, and he was named a "junior minister" (ministerial secretary) to the ministry of Mr. *X*, whom *A* described as a "party regular and friend of Nkrumah."

A's functions in the ministry included negotiation of procurement contracts for the ministry on behalf of *X*. In mid-1963, after *A* had negotiated his first set of contracts, he presented them to *X* for signature, and was asked if they were "the standard form of contract." *A* replied that he had followed all regulations in their preparation and negotiation. *X* then singled out a contract with a British firm and suggested that this and two other contracts, though technically valid, did not include the "usual commissions." "In fact," according to *A*, *X* "expressed surprise that the three contractors had not themselves mentioned the commissions." *X* indicated that in view of the expenses involved in maintaining ministries—including, notably, the periodic contributions they were required to make to the party—a "ministerial commission" was usually included in contract negotiations, although it was never written into the formal contract documents. *X* said that 10 percent of the net worth of the contract was the usual commission, to be paid in cash or the equivalent. If it was paid in cash, foreign exchange was preferred.

"I was somewhat surprised at all this, though I had heard that such things were done often." *A* then proceeded to "query about" and discovered that similar practices were common throughout the ministries. "In my ministry, the 10 percent was divided up so that the minister got half, 20 percent went to junior minister(s), 10 percent to go-betweens, 10 percent to the party secretary, and the rest to an 'open cash fund' kept by the minister for 'expenses.'" The "expenses," according to *A*, were to pay informers within the ministry (*A* claimed the minister paid several minor officials to report on the activities of his ranking subordinates), to provide gifts for influential visitors, and to help maintain two women who "decorated" *X*'s outer office. "After some soul-searching," said *A*, "I agreed to go along with all this, and while I was in office I took in a good deal." Pressed for an approximate figure for "a good deal," *A* thought he might have taken in about N₵30,000. *A* pointed out that this sum did not derive solely from "commissions"; among other things, he undertook several "treks" (bush tours)*, received gifts from various supplicants, and was periodically "gifted" by people for whom he had done favors and who circulated about his offices and made themselves available for odd tasks.

"After the [1966] coup I was up before the Z_____ Assets Commission, but it only uncovered a part of my worth. Besides, I'd spent much of the money." What did *A* do with his admittedly illicit proceeds? *A* now reminded the author that only 80 to 90 percent of these proceeds came to him in cash; he could assign no value to favors, "good turns," or various small gifts of goods, hardware, and edible animals. He also pointed out that it was difficult for him to separate his personal assets and his regular salary and perquisites from what he took in from "commissions" and the like. He thought, however, that "as memory serves," the N₵30,000 had been used in the following ways:

—To make the down payment on the purchase of a Mercedes-Benz automobile
—To buy furnishings for his home in Accra
—To defray most of the purchase price of a house and farm for himself in his home town
—To build a new house for his mother, and to furnish it completely with a bedstead, table, chairs, and a "fridge in the sitting room and a short-wave radio"

---

* The "bush tour", as it was commonly practiced during the Nkrumah and Busia eras, was a kind of pastoral journey made by ministers of government and other high officials, ostensibly to check on the progress of government-funded projects, ascertain development needs, identify problems, or reassure constituents. During the visits, the official or his aides were commonly "gifted" in cash, "drink," or edible animals. The value of the "gift" tended to vary from situation to situation, depending on the importance of the visitor, his hosts' desire to impress him, and the size and wealth of the place visited. In any case, the customary "gift" ranged in value between N₵100 and N₵500, and an enterprising minister could pick up as much as N₵3,000 on such a tour. It is not always clear what the donors got in return for their gifts—save promises—but the exchange was certainly both illegal and politically corrupt.

—To help his two brothers in their joint business

—To "gift" several Ghanaians who worked in some of the firms with which he had negotiated contracts (implying that these persons had acted as brokers in a number of transactions)

—As "annual gifts" to Minister X and as "contributions" to the party

—As "dash" to local officials with whom his family dealt, as well as customary "drink" (liquor or money) for the local chief

Mr. A was asked to pay the government a sum equivalent to those assets he could not properly account for at the time of his investigation, and by the time he was interviewed (December 1970–February 1971) he claimed he had already paid most of that sum.

Among the more interesting aspects of the interviews with Mr. A, apart from his frankness, were his recollections about the extent and ramifications of relationships he developed while he was in office and able to dispense political goods. Insofar as they can be generalized from his statements, his relationships tended to be directed to certain clusters of individuals distinguished according to two criteria: their operational relationship to the formal polity, and their functional relationship to A. (See Figure 1.) Within the polity were A's superiors, his equals, and two groups of his subordinates: major official subordinates (principally senior civil servants), and minor official subordinates (clerks, typists, etc.). Some of the members of the latter subordinate group had overlapping membership in the formal polity and the public sphere, i.e., in the group designated "entourage" in Figure 1. This cluster included not only several individuals who owed their official positions to A, but various expediters, brokers, "verandah boys", and other hangers-on. Outside the polity were A's family, some of whose members also belonged to the "entourage" and the minor official subordinates group; A's major clients (the contractors); and a residual category including various minor clients and supplicants. Finally, there was a somewhat more distant group, technically within the polity but geographically far from Accra, including local officials and chiefs with whom A occasionally dealt directly or indirectly (through his family).

Mr. A was asked if he could estimate the number of people who were either "regular" extra-legal recipients of "his" political goods or with whom he had "regular" informal transactions involving the unsanctioned exchange of political goods in his control for political or

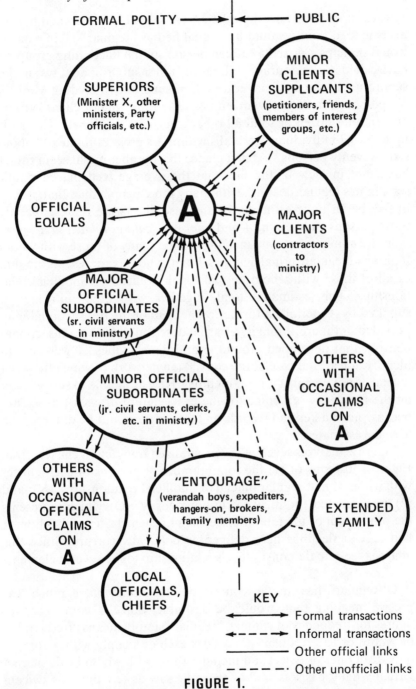

FIGURE 1.
Generalized Transactional Clusters for Mr. A, Former Ministerial Secretary

private goods controlled by others.* He said at least ten members of his extended family would have qualified as "regular" recipients; so would perhaps a dozen to fifteen persons in the fluctuating group we have called A's "entourage", about six minor subordinates, two major subordinates, three official equals, four superiors (including Minister X), perhaps fifteen to seventeen persons in the "major client" group, and another dozen or so in all other categories combined. This adds up to 65–67 individuals, and falls within A's gross estimate of "about sixty–seventy persons." At first glance this number might seem rather large, but in view of the fact that the average well placed public servant has regular dealings with many more people than that, it may in fact be an underestimate. In any case, the figure represents only those persons with whom A had *informal dealings related to his position*; the number certainly includes a great many of those with whom A also had regular formal dealings, but it in no way represents the sum of all of those with whom he had regular official or unofficial relationships. This estimated total, together with other information supplied by A, permits a further refinement of the transactional map provided in Figure 1, that is, a partial description of the transactional network that developed around A and his activities. A was able to identify at least the core of the conversion network of which he was a crucial, if not the most crucial member. He was unable to supply data on the frequency of contact or the exact nature of each transaction because he had kept no records on these matters and he did not wish to make estimates.

Figure 2 analyzes seven of the generalized transaction clusters from Figure 1 in terms of (1) the total number of persons in each cluster with whom A had regular official or unofficial relationships. (N); and (2) the estimated "political corruption density" (D), which represents the proportion of the total number within each cluster with whom A had regular dealings here defined as politically corrupt. Since this analysis seeks to demonstrate A's relationship to the several elements

* "Regular" has, in the context of this discussion, a much less precise meaning than would be desirable. Since A could give no figures for frequency of contact, "regular" simply means "frequently" or "more or less frequently." It does exclude people with whom he only dealt once or twice, and includes those with whom he dealt on a virtually daily basis as well as those he saw as few times as twice a month.

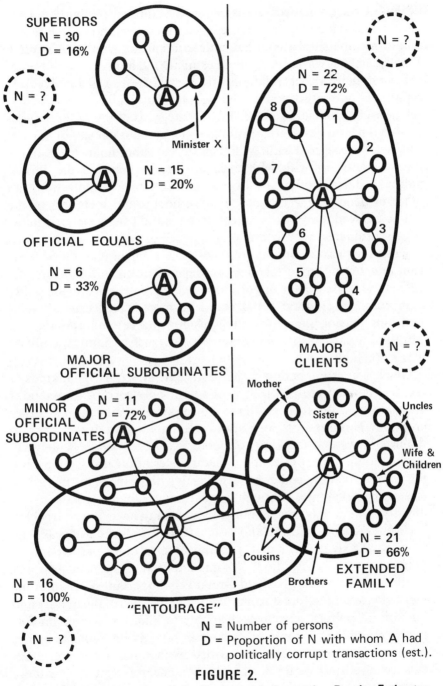

FIGURE 2.

Mr. A: Regular Transactions, by Cluster, with Corruption Density Estimates of the conversion network, A is depicted as the central figure in each cluster. No N and D estimates are given for clusters shown in Figure 1 whose membership was either indeterminate or dim in A's mind. Finally, since it was impossible to estimate the human population of the *total* network of relationships in which A was involved, D represents only a portion of the people with whom A had regular relationships, official or unofficial. On the basis of the limited quantifiable data, however, it appears that the greatest density of corrupt transactions occurred with/within clusters at subordinate levels in the formal polity, or with/within those generally outside the formal polity. A did not offer any explanation for this concentration, but other evidence suggests that (a) subordinates and members of the public enjoyed more ready access to A than did superiors or equals; (b) subordinates, who commanded fewer or lesser resources than equals or superiors, were more vulnerable to manipulation or coercion and by the same token more dependent on A for favors; (c) clientage and patronage opportunities were greater outside the polity than within the polity; (d) A could be more selective in his relationships outside the polity than inside; and (e) subordinate and extra-polity clusters included many persons (such as family members) who stood high in A's hierarchy of trust.[6]

One last question before we leave the case of Mr. A: What kinds of political goods were involved in A's politically corrupt transactions and did they differ from cluster to cluster, or according to some other criterion? This question can be answered only in part. It is clear from the interviews that the kinds of goods exchanged varied widely according to the time, place, and circumstances of the transactions, but no general pattern could be discerned with respect to any given cluster. For example, although a great many tangible goods flowed directly or indirectly to A's family, they seem to have flowed freely to his friends, clients, patrons, and associates in the other clusters as well.

To what extent is A's case generalizable to other participants in Ghana's political corruption? In some important respects he was not, a typical office-holder. He held a relatively important position in the hierarchy, and therefore it seems likely that in terms of the quality and quantity of political resources available to him, his case might formally resemble only those of persons in roughly the same or higher positions. Yet, given the data provided by the other twelve respondents surveyed in chapter 3, plus the evidence of some of the more detailed reports from the Commissions of Inquiry, these points seem to have general validity at all levels of officialdom: (a) individual transactions lie at the base of politically corrupt behavior; (b) transactions do seem to fall into clusters of individuals who are identifiable by their position within the polity, or more generally, by their functional relationships to officials who occupy pivotal positions in the corruption process; (c) "density" appears to be related to the nature of the position occupied by the official dispensing largesse, i.e., whether he occupies a "line" position (as did *A*) or a "staff" position.[7] Thus, position appears to determine the individual's opportunity for engaging in corrupt practices and to define the clusters with whom he might engage in transactions. The case of Mr. *A*, therefore, though atypical because the subject held a relatively high position in the formal polity, nonetheless epitomizes a significant range of possible corrupt relationships.

Other, less formal generalizations can be derived from data on individual instances of political corruption, particularly from the reports on the Jiagge, Manyo-Plange, and Sowah commissions, which were appointed by the NLC to look into the assets of various governmental and CPP figures. These three inquiries yielded a mine of documented detail that both confirms and supplements the information derived from our twelve interviewees.

In all, the three assets commissions inculpated more than one hundred persons in the acquisition of income or assets well in excess of the amounts their legitimate salaries and investments would have brought them during their terms in office. To be sure, that number is by no means inclusive; the nets cast for the assets inquiries brought in only some of the bigger fish and for various reasons missed most of the host of lesser figures investigated by other commissions. Further, it is certain that the assets or income that came under scrutiny by the assets commissions represented only a relatively small proportion of the total take illegally realized by those under investigation. For one thing, the rules of evidence adopted by the commissions tended to resolve any legal doubts in favor of the persons named,* and for

---

* The assets commissions stipulated, for example, that a property would be liable to confiscation only if it could be proved that more than 50 percent of its capital worth came from illicit or unaccounted sources. Thus, some houses and land acquired under extremely questionable circumstances remained in the hands of their owners because the "over 50 percent" rule could not be squarely applied.

another, much vital information on income and expenditures was simply unavailable. Even so, the reports on these inquiries do give a vivid picture of the life styles and spending patterns of a good many politicians of the Nkrumah period. Three points in particular emerge from these documents.

First, it is patent that many CPP politicians found in government or Party, or both, extraordinary opportunities for self-enrichment at public expense. The judgments rendered by the assets commissions—for money or property to be recovered by the state—give some indication of the extent of that enrichment. For example, the twenty-one persons against whom the Jiagge Commission rendered judgments were required to pay to the state an aggregate sum of 1,325,320 New Cedis (N₵; $1.00 = N₵1.02). The judgments ranged from a high of N₵653,739.27 (for Krobo Edusei, a former minister) to a low of N₵1,108.75 (for Lucy Anin, a former member of Parliament). Most were above N₵5,000, and indeed the majority ran to five or six figures: A. E. Inkumsah (ex-minister, Deputy Speaker), was required to pay N₵124,666.23; Komlah Gbedemah (ex-minister), N₵35,929.80; B. E. Kwaw-Swanzy (ex-minister), N₵17,030.35; A. H. B. Suleimana (ex-MP, CPP official), N₵12,326.26; J. E. Hagan (ex-MP, Regional Commissioner), N₵53,480.80; E. Tachie-Menson (ex-minister), N₵45,171.27; F. K. D. Goka (ex-minister), N₵56,121.07; Salifu Yakubu (ex-MP, CPP official), N₵15,714.91; Sulemana K. Tandoh (ex-ambassador, MP), N₵12,589.50; A. K. Puplampu (ex-minister), N₵112,261.90; M. Appiah-Danquah (ex-minister, ambassador, secretary-general of the United Ghana Farmers' Cooperatives Council), N₵82,374.57; G. Y. Odoi (former general manager of the Cocoa Purchasing Company, manager of GNCC), N₵27,925.10; E. C. D. Asiama (ex-director of the Research Bureau of the Ministry of External Affairs), N₵51,793.27.[8]

Those who realized such extra income, it need hardly be added, could support a relatively luxurious life style. In addition to business investments, their expenditures tended to be divided between the purchase of real estate (some of it in Britain), and outlays for expensive consumer goods—notably cars, radios, furniture, and major kitchen appliances such as stoves and refrigerators. According to Richard Rathbone, who studied a group of eighteen CPP politicians, "there was a rapid succession of cars; in 1964 the. . . politicians in the sample owned between them forty-one cars, including fourteen Mercedes-Benz saloons and six Chevrolets and Cadillacs."[9] Girl friends likewise must be accounted an important manifestation of conspicuous consumption, for, unlike most of their counterparts in Europe and the United States, they were kept in open and elegant display, languidly adorning the outer offices of ministerial suites or the back seats of expensive automobiles. Here the relationship between Nkrumah and Genoveva Marais perhaps set the tone: if the President could parade his mistresses, so could others in the top echelons. In the real estate league, Krobo Edusei appears to have been the champion. He acquired no less than twenty-seven houses and rented several of them for extra income. Not far behind were Messrs. I. B. Asafo-Agyei (who owned fourteen houses, and rented eight of them) and Emmanuel Ayeh-Kumi (who had twelve houses, of which four were rented). Finally, the houses the politicians occupied tended themselves to inspire a great deal of conspicuous consumption. Mrs. Edusei's acquisition of a golden bed has already been noted;[10] other politicians may not have attracted so much notoriety by their purchases, but certainly some were no less generous in their expenditures. A good example is that of A. E. Inkumsah (a former minister), as reported by the Jiagge Assets Commission:

> Mr. Inkumsah furnished house No. C890/4 at Kokomlemle and house No. 23/4, Palm Land Estate, Sekondi, very lavishly and used them as his residence[s] in Accra and Sekondi.

> A lot of furniture of the Louis XIV period style was imported from Italy for these houses. . . . [In the Sekondi house] The dining room table was eight feet by 4 feet. One bed measured 8 feet by 7 feet. The sideboard had a marble top. There were three bedroom suites, a dining room suite and a lounge suite. There were magnificent settees, an American bar, a strong room with a steel door, a steel safe and several other items all equally luxurious.

> The total amount of furniture purchased from the Ghana Italian Furniture Company *alone* was £ 8,151. . . .[11]

A second point that emerges from the assets inquiries is that the politicians showed great enterprise in maximizing the new income opportunities to which their positions gave them access. A good many were small businessmen and contractors before they went into politics in the mid-fifties; these men simply continued and expanded their business activities while in public office. In addition, many who came to government from the civil service and professional ranks started businesses while they were in office.

The most common business activity was the renting of houses. Other forms of enterprise included: selling schoolbooks (Preko, ex-minister), hiring out dump trucks (Preko, Puplampu, Asafo-Agyei, and Amoa-Awuah, all ex-ministers), operating fisheries (Asafo-Agyei and Puplampu), cocoa farming (Asafo-Agyei), poultry farming (Kwaw-Swanzy and Gbedemah, ex-ministers), hog breeding (Ayeh-Kumi, financial advisor to Nkrumah), food-crop farming (Preko and Asafo-Agyei), hotel management (Batsa, party ideologist), raising cattle (Igala, ex-minister) operating grocery shops (Ayeh-Kumi) and fish shops (Adamafio, former CPP secretary-general), interior decoration (Ayeh-Kumi), transport (Amoa-Awuah), supplying rocks for the construction of Tema harbor (Andoh, managing director of NADECO), investment in the Ashanti Turf Club (Asafo-Agyei), and selling cattle (Yakubu, ex-MP and CPP official).[12] The list is merely representative, not exhaustive; various government and CPP officials also held stock and directorships in large private businesses, some maintained businesses through third parties (most often relatives), and a great many indulged in some form of money-lending or financial speculation.

A third generalization that seems indicated by the evidence of the assets inquiries is that at the top echelons, the older party "militants" were somewhat more likely to be involved in political corruption, than the new "socialist boys,"[13] although corrupt activities among members of the latter group certainly are not hard to find.

We turn now to a documented case involving a number of persons who operated within one institutional setting, the former Ghana Football Pools Authority, which was investigated by a Committee of Inquiry during 1966-68. The unusually detailed report of that committee,[14] issued in 1971, permits further analysis of the process of political corruption at both the core- and extended- process levels.

The Case of the Football Pools Authority

Betting on the outcome of soccer matches played in the United Kingdom has long provided the rationale for the football pools that have proved highly profitable enterprises in almost all former British colonies and possessions. Indeed, betting on the matches is so popular in these areas of Africa that many territories, such as Nigeria, have maintained their own pools systems almost since the time they attained independence. Such "nationalization" of the football pools has enlarged the scope of the betting to accommodate matches played by local teams in local leagues. Primarily, however, it was carried out to curtail the large drain on foreign exchange reserves that resulted from the British management monopoly.

In 1960, Ghanaian Minister of Finance F. K. D. Goka proposed that his government enter into agreements with British pools companies with a view to getting a share of the profits accruing from their activities in Ghana. In January 1961 the Cabinet approved the establishment of a government-controlled central authority (the Ghana Football Pools Authority) to operate on a commission basis as sole general agent for all U. K. pools operating in Ghana. What this meant on a practical level was that all pools transactions were now handled through the Authority's administration and its licensed agents. The U. K. firms sent weekly negatives or films of their lists of scheduled soccer matches—i.e., their "tickets" or stakers' coupons (which the investigating committee's report termed "the lifeblood of the whole business")—and the coupons themselves were printed in Ghana and then distributed to sub-agents by the Authority's main agents. Bettors marked their coupons in duplicate and forwarded one copy to the Authority. At the end of each week, the sub-agents sent all the money they had collected (minus agreed commissions) to the main agents, together with lists showing the stakers' names and the amount staked by each. The main agents, in turn, deducted their own commissions and passed along the remaining sums, together with the sub-agents' lists, to the Authority. The Authority was responsible for forwarding the marked coupons and the moneys to the various pools firms in Britain. Winnings, of course, also were channeled back through the Authority.[15] Ostensibly, the entire process was regulated by written agreements between the U.K. firms and the Authority. Corrupt practices became commonplace, however, as winnings were received at the Authority and routed to bettors, and as commissions claimants proliferated as a result of informal arrangements developed within the Authority.

At the time the Authority was created, one Thomas Kanbi, a self-professed expert on pools matters who had been instrumental in

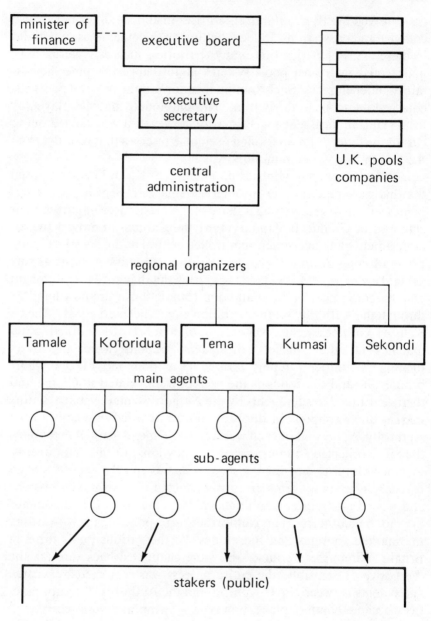

FIGURE 3. Organization of the Ghana Football Pools Authority

getting the proposal before the government, was appointed its acting general manager. Four regional organizers were named to work with him, one of whom, P. H. Amegashie, was to figure prominently in the Authority's later activities. Within four months, it became known that Kanbi had formed his own pools company (Kwob Pools); in light of this disclosure and numerous complaints from both the British pools firms and the public, Kanbi was charged with mismanaging the affairs of the Authority and suspended from duty (he was dismissed in July that year). An Interim Management Committee ran the Authority until May 1962, when the Cabinet approved the appointment of what amounted to a three-man executive board to run the Authority. Chairman of the board was Mr. A. K. Owona-Agyeman, then deputy minister in the Ministry of Finance and Trade, who had also been chairman of the Interim Committee. S. D. Asihene, the nominee of the state-run National Lotteries, was the second member of the board. The third member was a Mr. C. C. Y. Onny, sitting as the representative of the principal secretary of the Ministry of Finance; Onny was later replaced by S. E. Arthur (neither Onny nor Arthur was ever implicated in corruption). This group ran the Authority until April 1965, when the Authority and the Department of National Lotteries were absorbed into a new body, the State Lotteries Corporation, and Owona-Agyeman's administration came to an end. Owona-Agyeman's successor, W. F. Brennan, discovered numerous irregularities in the operation of the Authority and thereupon secured the removal of S. D. Asihene (who had been the effective day-to-day administrator of the Authority between 1962 and 1965). Brennan also submitted a detailed report to the minister of finance, who took up the matter in the Cabinet on October 28, 1965. The Brennan report, together with a report subsequently issued by the Cabinet, apparently sparked the later investigations undertaken by an NLC–created Committee of Enquiry.[16]

These are the outlines of the short history of the Football Pools Authority from its creation in 1961 until its incorporation into a larger body in 1965. During the four years of its autonomous life it appears to have operated somewhat on the margins of government, apparently causing few of the ripples in the busy pool of Ghanaian political life. In one respect, however, it was hardly a marginal operation: between 1962 and 1965 it took in more than £ 500,000 in commissions on a gross take that probably exceeded £ 4,000,000 from the sale of several hundred thousand football coupons.[17] It handled winnings ranging from ten shillings to thousands of pounds (in one case over £ 17,000), and through its various agents and sub-agents it was involved with literally thousands of Ghanaians who hoped to strike it rich by correctly predicting the outcomes of soccer matches played in England. More to the point, the Authority began as an enterprise in larceny—under Kanbi—and behind the shield of government disinterest it was able to develop into a well organized network for institutionalized political corruption. In the words of the investigating committee:

> The administration of the Football Pools Authority during the period under review portrays a classic example of how a government institution was, metaphorically speaking, held as a parsimony [sic; the committee meant "patrimony"] by those who had been entrusted to run its affairs. Nepotism was rife in the appointments to fill the key positions and salary increases were awarded in a manner which could be described as whimsical; audit queries which were meant as potions to cure the ills in the administration were disregarded and left unanswered; the Minister of Finance was left an uninformed outsider in those important transactions of the Authority where his sanction ought to have been sought; the provisions of the parent Act which were to give legality to the conduct of the Authority's affairs were set at nought. . . . In our view the Minister's apparent nonchalance mainly fostered this sad situation.[18]

It would serve little purpose to examine in detail the large number of corrupt acts revealed by the Committee of Inquiry.* It is important

---

* A general enumeration, however, may be enlightening (numerals refer to main paragraphs in the report): irregular use of Authority staff time for the personal benefit of commissioned agents (79–81); collection of commissions on fictitious agents (89–92); unauthorized collection of tickets from printers by main agents, leading to possible collusion and fraud in the distribution of unrecorded tickets (96–97); collusive overcharges in printing contracts (98, 99); failure of main agents to pay income tax or commissions on staked tickets (100, 101); insertion of staked but unpaid coupons in batches sent to the United Kingdom (104–106); irregular, irrational,

to note that these acts involved persons at every level of the Authority's hierarchy (see Figure 3) and furthermore included dealings with a variety of clients, contractors, and other interested parties outside the formal polity. Of particular note are the activities of the Authority's managers, who not only set the tone of permissiveness in which corrupt activities were countenanced as normal practice, but personally initiated or actively abetted much of the organization's corruption. "Patrimony" is certainly an apt description of the manner in which they ran the Authority. It is known that Asihene put a brother, a half brother, three cousins, and several other unspecified relatives on the payroll in key positions, and that Owona-Agyeman similarly placed his father-in-law, a half brother, and four other relatives. Moreover the evidence suggests that even more of the relatives of these two directors found employment in lesser positions in the Authority; during the 1961–65 period employees were hired in large numbers, many of them directly by or through the intercession of the two directors. One of Asihene's cousins, Twum-Asihene, an accountant who rose to the position of acting executive secretary in

---

unauthorized, and nepotistic recruitment practices (107–142); payment of double salaries (146–148); irregular salary increases (168); illegal conversion of sterling remittance (176–207); failure to record sterling remittances and suppression of their covering letters (208–210); taking of bribes (214–221); irregular salary advances and allowances granted to staff (22–236); possible collusion in a failure to collect a debt owed to the Authority (243–246); various faulty accounting procedures conducive to or associated with fraudulent practices such as false reporting of profits, cashing a check known to be forged, double collection on staked tickets, and misappropriation of funds (260–334); various questionable and sometimes illicit dealings with coupon printers, notably the Liberty Press and its owner, Mr. Kumi (335–354); possible bribery of Asihene by Kumi (355–358); and outright misappropriation of small winnings checks (366–370). This list does not include various administrative improprieties noted in the report, nor does it reflect the ways in which repeated violations of the regulations and laws governing the Authority contributed to the climate of relaxed indifference within the Authority, which in turn made acts of political corruption seem both normal and acceptable.

the Authority, was described by the Committee of Inquiry as an "asset to the organization." Other such appointments did not fare so well, doubtless because many of them involved relatives who turned out to be inefficient or incompetent, or both.

Also of interest to this study is the working relationship between Owona-Agyeman, Asihene, and P. H. Amegashie (a member of the first Interim Management Committee who later served as acting executive secretary and then, after a falling-out with the first two, became regional organizer at Tema). These three men were able to construct a highly profitable set of transactional networks through their control of appointments and by manipulation of the considerable resources at their disposal. The family appointments seem to have been one of the keys to the network, so much so that (in the words of the Committee report), "It was complained that the way and manner Mr. Owona-Agyeman and Mr. S. D. Asihene. . . were appointing their relatives to the Authority created the impression the organization was being run on a family basis."[19]

One major benefit of the close interrelationship between Owona-Agyeman, Asihene, Amegashie, and their appointees was that it facilitated the illegal conversion of sterling checks that were issued to local winners. For example, in one case, the Committee of Inquiry inculpated Amegashie in the conversion of a "£ 100– £ 200" check (which the official used to buy goods in London); in another incident, Amegashie and Asihene converted checks totaling £ 800 (Asihene allegedly used part of this sum for the purchase of a Mercedes-Benz car). Furthermore, Owona-Agyeman and Asihene were held jointly responsible for the conversion of a £ 17,082 sterling check which "found its way into Mr. Owona-Agyeman's pocket", and in two other cases Owona-Agyeman was blamed for converting sterling checks in the amounts of £ 1,060 and £ 2,035.[20] It appears that these acts of peculation were possible because (a) all winnings had not only to pass through the Authority's central administration but to come before the notice of the directors (this presumably to satisfy exchange control regulations); (b) Amegashie for a time was responsible for opening all mails containing remittances, a task for which, by his own admission, he kept no records; (c) supervision by the Ministry of Finance and the Auditor-General's Office was either "nonchalant" (to use the report's term) or could simply be ignored; and (d) in the eyes of the Authority's principals, everybody was doing it:

Mr. Amegashie . . . had himself readily admitted that he indulged in such dishonest conversion of foreign checques, but that it was the common practice. It was alleged that Mr. Owona-Agyeman was, to Mr. S. D. Asihene's knowledge, also guilty of this practice.[21]

Again, the full details of these transactions need not detain us; what must be stressed is that most of them required the active collaboration of various subordinates in the Authority—accountants, secretaries, clerks, and the like. Since many of these persons owed their positions to Owona-Agyeman and Asihene, it is easy to see how they could be readily induced to collaborate in these and other corrupt transactions. It is perhaps significant that although the Committee of Inquiry's report records much denial of guilt and many attempts to lay blame elsewhere, none of the witnesses denied knowledge of the basic situation described by the Committee's report; in fact, a number readily admitted at least qualified involvement and, like Amegashie, suggested that the Authority's activities were not unusual when seen in context. If our analysis of Ghana's incipient culture of political corruption is at all persuasive, their point was well taken.

A Ghanaian Informal Polity?

The model of political corruption advanced in chapter 1 posits an "informal polity" as a possible outgrowth of the extended process of political corruption, given two principal conditions antecedent: (1) the existence of a culture of political corruption, and (2) the growth and generalization of corrupt informal networks connected to a "formal" polity though themselves perhaps only rudimentarily interconnected. Since coherence among the networks would tend to strengthen relationships on all sides and since it appears that members of the networks tend to seek durable connections (particularly if they find that such associations provide high rewards), a relatively high degree of inter-network cohesion can be expected under certain conditions. The conditions appear to have been particularly favorable for this kind of cohesion in Sicily, where the Mafia long ago succeeded in consolidating its power, and in Indonesia during the "Guided Democracy" period of Sukarno's rule. But these examples suggest the existence of an illegal system that parallels the formal polity, an informal polity that has achieved almost governmental power and authority. That clearly was not the direction in which the Ghanaian system was moving in the 1960s and the early 1970s.

Nor was the Ghanaian situation simply a reflection of the interplay of assorted "parapolitical" arenas, those political structures which, according to F. G. Bailey, function at the subnational level in villages, professional associations, universities, political factions, etc.; "which are partly regulated by, and partly independent of, larger encapsulating political structures; and which ... fight battles with these larger structures in a way which for them seldom ends in victory, rarely in dramatic defeat, but usually in a long drawn stalemate and defeat by attrition."[22] This is not to say that such parapolitical systems did not exist in Ghana in the period under survey. On the contrary, they were a very real part of the total system, and indeed, as our model anticipates, many of them had produced their own extended networks of political corruption, each defined according to the formal structural givens of the situation. In Nkrumah's Ghana, government corporations, municipal councils, the Trades Union Council, even the CPP, tended to operate as parapolitical systems, though more often than not (after 1963) without the impediment of permanent conflict with encapsulating structures. Moreover, Maxwell Owusu's study of Agona-Swedru admirably describes politics in what must be seen as one such system operating on a wider basis and at a lower level.[23] But the presence of all these parapolitical systems does not, per se, indicate the existence of an informal polity in Ghana. Indeed it may merely indicate that the meaning of the term "sub-system" needs to be broadened in the Ghanaian context, and the hardly startling conclusion that Ghanaian politics reflect the interests of a wide variety of parochial political arenas and factional sets.[24]

A Ghanaian informal polity, then, if one has ever existed, cannot be sought solely at the developmental extreme of our model, in the realm of parapolitical systems. Rather, it is only by standing back from the detail of previous discussions and viewing the system with particular reference to the two conditions previously noted (existence of a culture of political corruption, and endogenous, parallel networks) that we can achieve a more enlightening perspective.

We have already documented the growth of a culture of political corruption in Ghana. The evidence further indicates the presence of networks of political corruption both within and growing out of the structures of the formal polity. Taken together, these findings suggest the minimal conditions were at hand for the development of an informal polity (or polities). What is lacking is evidence of linkage between networks of corruption. We argue that the evidence exists, but that it tends to be "soft" evidence, i.e., circumstantial and inferential (from the data of the Commissions of Inquiry and from several studies of the Ghanaian political system).

At the formal level, probably the most visible instrument of national linkage was the CPP, which attained a virtual identity with the state following the 1963 constitutional referendum on the one-party state. Through its operating parts, plus its women's, youth, and trade-union auxiliaries, it strove to become a party of mass mobilization. Almost all authorities on Ghanaian politics agree, however, that it never realized that goal. Fitch and Oppenheimer accurately reflect the consensus on this point:

> The CPP was a mass party only in the sense that it had a large membership. It was not a mass party in the sense of mobilizing large numbers of people and bringing them into the political arena as active and politically conscious participants.[25]

More to our point, the party did operate as a channel for political and economic preferment, for the amassing of private wealth, and for the creation of diverse schemes designed to reap profit for its numerous political entrepreneurs. In one sense the CPP truly was a mobilizing party: it mobilized a great deal of the public and private wealth of the country for the benefit of the political elite.[26] Dennis Austin put the case squarely: "[The CPP] had always been corrupt: but it had also fought for self-government. Now however that the political kingdom was complete, the opportunities for private gain were very great."[27] At local levels the party required party membership of practically everyone who sought dealings with the government; for example, membership in the CPP was required for farmers who hoped to qualify for loans from the CPP-administered Cocoa Purchasing Company. "This principle," state Fitch and Oppenheimer, "was systematically extended to nearly every government agency."[28] Petty party officials "used the names of persons in prominent positions to collect money for themselves";[29] party militants were preferred in the allocation of such valuable local political goods as public offices and market stalls;[30] and local party officials and memberships developed a variety of techniques for extorting money and favors from business-men, market-women, civil servants, and the like, in exchange for "protection" and other "benefits." At the higher levels, as we have noted, the opportunities for exerting influence were commensurately more lucrative, wide-ranging and easily seized. In both formal and informal ways, therefore, the party reached into virtually every corner of Ghana's public life and provided, through its officials at all levels, both horizontal and vertical linkages within the system. Clearly, also, the key men in the party—be they of the old "right wing" that was partially discredited in 1961, or of the "left wing", which for a time gained ascendancy after 1961 under the leadership of Party Secretary-General Tawia Adamafio[31]—played crucial linkage roles in the widespread networks of corruption in which the party was involved. Thus the party supplied at least some of the cement for an informal polity in Ghana.

A second, perhaps equally important set of linkages was inherent in the relationships, both formal and informal between Nkrumah and his principal economic and financial advisers, between various government units and the Ghanaian business community, and between all these interests and the several secretariats that controlled such entities as the state corporations and in turn were controlled (after 1964) by the president. This large and somewhat ponderous aggregation contributed many of the most important components in a system of intermeshing networks of corruption that were all concerned, in one way or another, with the exploitation and allocation of the country's economic resources. Two of the units in the set, the State Enterprises Secretariat and NADECO, best exemplify the nature of the formal and informal linkages under consideration.

By March, 1965, forty-seven state enterprises had been created. The Boards, as one quick glance at the rosters showed, had been staffed not with the most competent but with the most loyal . . . friends and associates of the President, including a number of attractive but totally inexperienced women members of the National Assembly. Since these establishments were directly under the presidential State Enterprises Secretariat, headed by all-purpose Executive Secretary J. V. Phillips, thousands of employees and millions of pounds were at the President's mercy and disposal. They were no farther from his personal control than the nearest telephone. The efficiency-oriented staff members in the Secretariat who attempted to half the drift to institutionalized incompetence and corruption were fighting a losing battle.[32]

The above summary, from Henry Bretton's study of Nkrumah, reflects its author's view that both the state and party apparatuses were handmaidens of Nkrumah's personal rule. Bretton may have pushed that point a bit too far, but he is unquestionably correct in his appraisal of the recruitment and appointment procedures used to fill key positions in the state boards and corporations. There was, for example, the Ghana Cargo Handling Company, a joint-stock state corporation whose managing director, H. K. Biney, apparently took direct control of the company through Nkrumah's personal intervention and over the opposition of key civil servants who were finally instructed to "keep hands off" the company and its operations. Biney's administration, if the Commission of Inquiry that investigated the company is to be believed, was notable for its mismanagement, financial malpractice, and recruitment irregularities. Of interest here is not only the company's patently close relationship to Nkrumah (through Biney) but its informal links to the CPP. According to the investigating commission,

No direct or indirect evidence was adduced before the Commission which connected the Ghana Cargo Handling Company with the Convention People's Party in any way. It is only the hectoring but muffled presence of the Party that was felt in the Organization. Even though the Company is a limited liability one and autonomous in all respects, it appears that it was influenced by the Party indirectly in the choice of the personnel of its employees. Anybody regarded by the Party as *persona non grata* was to be anathema to the Company and must be hounded out if already employed.[33]

The situation was much the same, to a greater or lesser degree, in most of the other state boards and corporations. Links between party and government echelons permitted formal and informal penetration of virtually all agencies of the state by members of the new elite, and many of these bureaucratic newcomers used their positions to create their own corruption networks (as in the case of the Football Pools

Authority) or to reinforce and develop informal networks already in existence.

NADECO, as we have seen, presented a particularly flagrant example of high-level, formal-informal linkage agencies within the system. The Azu Crabbe Commission, which investigated the affairs of NADECO, summarized some of the links and their manner of operation:

> In order to sustain the flow of money the CPP became an agent for NADECO Ltd., for, according to the evidence, a considerable volume of business was introduced to NADECO Ltd. by the CPP. The CPP itself was the Government of Ghana, and Ministers of the Government saw to it that NADECO Ltd., as far as was practicable, became the agent in any business concern over which the government had control. For example, on 24th April, 1961, the Minister of Finance directed that all means of transport purchased with an advance from public funds should, as long as any amount of the advance was outstanding, be insured through the agency of NADECO Ltd. Principal Secretaries, Heads of Departments and Secretaries to Regional Commissioners to whom the directions were addressed were to ensure that when applications for advances for means of transport were received in their offices, the insurance company quoted should be NADECO Ltd. The Accountant-General was also instructed to pay the premiums directly to NADECO Ltd. A similar directive was addressed to all Statutory Boards, Corporations, and Local Authorities, and Principal Secretaries responsible for these bodies were also similarly directed to ensure that payment of premiums were made directly to NADECO Ltd.
>
> There is also evidence that on 26th April, 1961, the Minister of Trade directed that with effect from 1st May, 1961, arrangements should be made for NADECO Ltd. to provide transport for the distribution of Cocoa Marketing Board bags to the various buying centres. It was further directed by the Minister that as from the same date the handling of Cocoa Marketing Board cocoa at Takoradi should be undertaken by NADECO Ltd.[34]

According to the Azu Crabbe Commission, NADECO's financial links extended as well to other government bodies. The Ghana National Construction Company (originally a joint Israeli-Ghanaian enterprise, later solely Ghanaian) and the State Housing Corporation, both prime intermediaries between the government and important public works contractors (which included, notably, the expatriate firms of Parkinson-Howard and A. Lang), apparently contributed large sums to and through NADECO, some of which were either derived corruptly or flowed into corrupt channels with the knowledge of all concerned. The Ghana Educational Trust (an endowment set up with funds from the Cocoa Marketing Board with the purpose of building schools), the Ghana Cargo Handling Company, the Ghana Bottling Company, the Ghana Industrial Development Corporation, a vaguely defined group known as the Newspapers Distribution Company, Ltd., as well as the Cocoa Marketing Board, were some of the other public and quasi-public organizations with direct, and in these cases corrupt, links to NADECO. Most important, NADECO, through its agents and directors (of whom the most important was Emmanuel Ayeh-Kumi, one of Nkrumah's most trusted advisors and "bribe collectors"—to use the Commission's terms) reached virtually every major private Ghanaian and expatriate concern that had any contractual and financial dealings with the government. The list of expatriate concerns involved in these transactions is extremely long, and includes not only the firms mentioned previously (Zim, Parkinson-Howard, Gilbey's, A. G. Leventis, Henschel), but the Société Commerciale de l'Ouest Africain (SCOA; an important French wholesaling and distribution group), Africa Motors (Britain), and Phillips (Netherlands).

It would serve little purpose to detail further the evidence of major formal and informal linkages in the system. Close reading of the reports of the Commissions of Inquiry reveals many, many more. What is now of importance is whether such linkages constitute proof of an informal polity, as our model describes it. The evidence, again, is by and large "soft", and certainly is not in itself sufficient to make the case for the existence of a Ghanaian informal polity. Yet, it is sufficient to suggest that by 1965 the outlines of a national informal polity had begun to emerge, particularly if the members of the CPP-government elite, in their ramified and diverse legal and extralegal activities, are viewed as primary points of linkage for the informal networks in being at the time. What permits this conclusion is the fact that many of the networks had become visible by 1965, and some of them clearly had become institutionalized through NADECO, the party, and certain of the private and quasi-public business enterprises that were run by top members of the elite. It can also be asserted —although this development is not central to our analysis—that some of the "parapolitical" systems (local governments and the like) had developed their own informal polities, usually with links to the larger networks operating on the national scene.

— 5 —

Causes and Consequences

Thus far, in presenting a descriptive, process-centered argument, we have only suggested some of the consequences of Ghanaian political corruption and we have deliberately avoided discussion of its causes. The reasons are two-fold: first, these matters are best examined against the background provided in the preceding chapters; and second, questions of cause and effect raise sensitive problems of data limitation and analysis that are best considered separately. Now, confining our analysis to the themes and topics of this study, we shall discuss causes in three contexts of particular relevance to political corruption in Ghana: corruption in traditional societies, the relationship between the growth of corruption in Ghana and the rise of the "new men," and several institutional-structural factors associated with the phenomenon. A brief examination of some of the Ghanaian consequences of corruption concludes the chapter.

The Search for Causes

The search for the causes of political corruption has never been an idle academic pursuit. Most analysts have assumed that an understanding of the root causes of corruption may lead to ways to overcome it, or at least to curtail its practices and mitigate its effects to such a degree that it no longer poses a threat to orderly public life. The logic of this assumption is simple: if corruption is a disease of the body politic, then correct diagnosis—which means understanding causes, workings, and effects—can lead to a cure. James C. Scott, for example, hints at a hope for such a cure in his recent comparative study of corruption: "The obstacles to a non-corrupt political order in less-

developed nations are real, but they are not insurmountable."[1] Harold
D. Lasswell, in his introduction to Syed Hussein Alatas' *The Sociology
of Corruption*, is more explicit. He commends the book particularly
"to those who will perceive in this discussion a fresh start in
comprehending and contributing to the eventual control of one of the
most recalcitrant characteristics of public and private life of yesterday
or today anywhere in the community of man."[2] Alatas himself underlines the antiquity of such aims in citing the efforts of an
eleventh-century Chinese minister of state, Wang An-shih, as well as
those of the celebrated Arab historian Ibn Khaldûn (1332–1406), both
active public officers who strove through an examination of causes to
prescribe remedies for political corruption.[3] Most significantly for our
discussion, the diagnosis-leads-to-cure assumption has clearly un-
derlain the creation and work of many commissions of inquiry into
corrupt practices in Ghana and elsewhere. The well known
Santhanam Committee, formed in 1962 to investigate instances of
corruption in Indian ministries and departments, was explicitly instructed not only to determine causes and effects but to provide a set of
curative recommendations.[4] Indonesia's Commission of Four, set up
by President Suharto in 1970, received a like charge, and even saw its
prescriptions enacted into law.[5]

The Anin commission, appointed in Ghana in 1970, also was
specifically charged with discovering the cause-effect-cure nexus
(however, it had issued only three interim reports by the end of 1972),
and it should be added that revelations of corrupt practices were
partially responsible for specific, remedial legislation in that country,
both before and after the 1966 coup.[6] But in Ghana, at least, statutes
appear to have had relatively little effect thus far on corruption. One
reason may be that in Ghana those charged with eliminating corruption were themselves tainted with it; indeed, under such circumstances, both investigations and remedial legislation tend to be
ineffective and pointless, or to become elaborate exercises in
hypocrisy. This is clearly the view held by Ghanaian novelist Ayi
Kwei Armah:

> There was a lot of noise, for some time, about some investigation
> designed to rid the country's trade of corruption. Designed by whom?
> Where were the people in power who were so uncorrupt them-
> selves? . . . The head of it was a professor from Legon. From Legon,
> they said, in order to give weight and seriousness to the enterprise. In

the end it was being said in the streets that what had to happen with all these things had happened. The net had been made in the special Ghanaian way that allowed the really big corrupt people to pass through it.[7]

If Kwei Armah's observations are right with respect to Ghana, they could have been made with equal validity about numerous other countries where investigations, regulations, and decrees have had as little effect on the incidence of corruption. Other reasons could be postulated, and more examples could be cited, but there is little need to belabor the obvious: the assumption concerning the diagnosis-cure linkage is incorrect insofar as it presupposes that the means and the will to effect remedies necessarily either exist in the polity or can be readily found. Whether those conditions can in fact be met of course depends entirely on circumstance particular to each polity.

Moreover, a search for causes poses formidable problems of analysis. One of the basic problems looms in the decision as to whether one ought to look for proximate or ultimate causes. If one opts for the former he tends to be plagued by doubts about whether his investigation has gone far enough to establish credible cause-and-effect connections, and if for the latter, he often confronts frustration in defining the scope of his analysis.[8] Another particularly vexing problem that bedevils the search for causes arises from the fact that the prevailing norms of a society (which determine that society's definition of corruption) are quite likely to change over time as a result of internal political and social dynamics.. Failure to perceive and account for such changes leads to a blurring of definitions, and sometimes invites what Heidenheimer calls "the easy moral judgments of citizens of more developed societies."[9]

Finally, we hold that the discovery of causes of corruption is in any case neither a necessary nor a sufficient condition to its prevention or cure. Given these qualifications, then, the proper inquiry is not of absolute causes, but toward a modified form of what Colin Leys has called "the central question for the scientific study of the problem: In any society, under what conditions is behaviour most likely to occur which a significant portion of the population will regard as corrupt?"[10] We ask: "Given varying circumstances of time, place, and prevailing norms, under what conditions has corruption become a political problem in Ghana?"

Traditional Contexts and the Effects of Colonialism

A number of analysts of corruption in Africa have argued that even though there may be a connection between certain traditional practices and contemporary corrupt behaviors, it would be wrong to link them causally. M. McMullan, for example, sees corruption as a consequence of a "clash" between old customs and new (colonial and post-colonial) forms of government; Ronald Wraith, Edgar Simpkins, and Ghanaian sociologist Ebow Mends contend that much of the corruption of recent times results from the abuse of customary practices, not from their carryover into new political contexts.[11] Many of the practices and customs in traditional societies that have been related to contemporary corruption involved payments of one kind or another—for example, in transactions connected with marriage or transfers of land or as payments made to chiefs by sub-chiefs and subjects. In traditional Ghanaian contexts, such payment might be made as "tokens" to seal a covenant, or, in the case of chiefs, to acknowledge political obligations or to give symbolic assurance of loyalty. Other usages that have been deemed relevant centered about gift-giving or tithing, for which a whole range of material and symbolic goods were provided as "services" due a chief, or a "stool" or "skin" (in Ghana, the symbols of chieftaincy or a chiefdom as distinct from the person of the chief himself). Mends and Prof. Busia both stress that although such practices might suggest parallels to bribery and corruption, they were not so considered in traditional contexts, and what is more, chiefly misuse of goods given as "service" rarely occurred because of the threat represented by a formidable array of checks and sanctions that could be invoked against the offending official. Normally, according to Busia, a "chief was wealthy in terms of the services he received, but he could not accumulate capital for his own personal use."[12]

Further, particularly in Ghana, certain traditions of exchanging gifts were mainly symbolic. The chief, for example, was expected to show largesse to members of his court and his subjects on various ceremonial occasions, and on such occasions he might order the distribution of "surplus"* tithes and gifts—traditionally such things as

---

* "Surplus" here means "in excess of that which a stool, by custom, was entitled to retain for its own use." I am told that all Ghanaian stools and skins operated under such restrictions.

palm wine, chickens, yams—to show his generosity and reinforce the aura of beneficence and well-being necessary to successful rule. His subjects in turn showed respect by offering symbolic gifts when they visited him or when he visited their villages. One form of such gifts, for example, was customary "drink": it could consist of yams or palm wine; more recently, "Kaiser" brand schnapps or even cases of beer have become acceptable. Again, argue the authorities, these practices as such did not constitute bribery or corrupt acts on the part of either donor or recipient; however, they contend, the perversion of these practices does add up to corruption—and this occurred principally during the colonial period.

The image of traditional systems as projected by these writers is persuasive insofar as it demonstrates the manner in which old practices were undermined in the colonial situation, lost their normative content, and were converted to purposes far removed from those prescribed by tradition. It is not entirely accurate in its near-idealization of chiefly virtue.

Certainly, most Ghanaian chiefs operated within the prescribed customary bounds, but on occasion chiefs were punished—even deposed—for misusing stool property, for misappropriating the property of subjects, or for committing acts that wasted, degraded, or otherwise violated communal political resources. For example, there is evidence that frequently, during succession disputes in which two or more families or individuals laid conflicting claim to a stool or skin, the principals actively competed in under-the-table gift-giving to persons involved in the final decision. Admittedly these are not matters often recorded, but there is evidence to suggest that greedy and even wicked leaders and chiefs were by no means unknown to traditional Ghanaian society, and that many of them got away with acts of misappropriation and extortion, however tight the customary curbs on power.[13] Moreover, zero-sum politics, very much a part of the traditional political picture in Ghana, sometimes fostered a "get it while you can" attitude among persons in power. In all, the image of political systems that remained without corruption until they encountered colonialism is somewhat misleading. A truer picture is likely to be much more complex, since it would combine the older realities with the wide range of social, economic, and political changes that were directly or indirectly related to European colonialism.

The effects of colonialism on traditional political systems have been treated at length in a diverse literature; only a few relevant points of general agreement will be noted here:[14]

1. European colonial governments, by introducing new, superordinate power relationships, undermined traditional authority systems at their most vulnerable points: status, deference, and obligatory service. Other impersonal institutions brought in by colonialism (churches, civil services, political parties, armies) had the same effect, since they tended to offer alternatives to institutions based on patrimonial, patron-client, or ethnic and kinship relationships.

2. As traditional loyalties were undermined, traditional power holders sought alternative sources of status in the values brought in by the new system, in the cash-mercantile nexus of the colonial economy or the manipulation of structures of indirect rule such as native treasuries. In Ghana, for example, chiefs acquired cocoa farms or went into business, and misappropriations from stool treasuries and native authority treasuries to pay private debts became relatively frequent, as did the practice of distributing bribes to electors when stools became vacant.[15]

3. Men who owed their position and status to the colonial situation, rather than to traditional sources, took advantage of changes in the political arena to manipulate customary expectations about obligation and service to their own advantage. For example, the "modern" Ghanaian politician who got his start during the colonial period readily learned to operate as a "big man," as an official or even a quasi-chief armed with the power of the state. In these guises he could "legitimately" demand traditional gifts for his services. The "bush tour" owed its origins to this development.

4. Insofar as the colonial government was regarded as alien and hence illegitimate, traditional restraints on misappropriation of state property could logically be disregarded.[16]

The above summary hardly does justice either to the literature or the subject; it is sufficient, however, to give weight to some modest conclusions. While it is obvious that political corruption in its contemporary forms did not exist in traditional Ghanaian contexts, the existence of elaborate sanctions against the misuse of political goods, together with the record of such abuses by traditional power holders, certainly suggests that Ghanaians were no strangers to acts later defined as politically corrupt; and it is patent that

Colonialism introduced not corruption, but sets of institutions, technologies, norms, and values alien to Africa. In the process of contact, the traditional definitions of political resources altered to incorporate, in a rather piecemeal, chaotic fashion, the political goods brought in by the colonial powers. [Amid] the complexities of this process of redefinition, incorporation, and adjustment . . . traditionally "august" figures became, very often, brokers in and manipulators of the new political resources, i.e., patronage, offices, loans, scholarships, and contracts. Their traditional clients, in return, gave them continued support, traditional legitimacy, perhaps taxes, and often votes where electoral systems were introduced. The magnates of northern Nigeria played this role, as did, with more or less success, the *ganwa* in Burundi, the *sheikhs* in Senegal, the *saza* chiefs of Buganda, as well as numbers of traditional chiefs in the Ivory Coast, Ghana, Niger, and Upper Volta. And, not unexpectedly, some exceeded both traditional and colonial norms in this new, mediatory role. . . . It is fair . . . to argue that among the reasons why some traditional "big men" could become brokers between their traditional constituencies and the emerging modern polities is the fact that they included as part of *their* political capital long-established patterns of status, deference, and expectations about traditional relationships. In the hands of ambitious traditional notables, or more recently, politicians, these patterns of deference, these expectations about traditional reciprocities could be exploited to create networks of informal relationships.[17]

Thus the connection between traditional politics and contemporary political corruption is not, admittedly, a causal one; the link lies in perceptions of what constitutes abuse of political office. The forms may have changed, the norms may have shifted, but in Ghana it is still thought reprehensible for a chief or any other man in public office to use the political goods entrusted him for private, unsanctioned purposes, the obligations of kinship and "cathartic conspicuous consumption"* notwithstanding. In this respect, at least, customary definitions of chiefly virtue and modern bureaucratic norms find a parallel.

---

* The phrase "cathartic conspicuous consumption" was suggested to me by Prof. Graft-Johnson of the Department of Sociology, University of Ghana. It refers to the consumption expected of "big men," by which their clients or constituents derive vicarious satisfaction from their good fortune. Despite widespread acceptance of the Protestant political ethic in Ghana, the modern "big man" who

The "New Men" in the Conquest of Political Power

Not only did traditional political values bend under the impact of colonialism, but the bureaucratic norms brought in by the colonial powers themselves began to warp as a consequence of social restructuring during the colonial period. In British Africa the operations of indirect rule were expected to provide, among other things, accommodation between traditional political norms and practices and the rational-bureaucratic institutions introduced by the British. The two systems were intended to co-exist to their mutual benefit, with the latter eventually (and quietly) absorbing the former in the natural course of events.[18] These self-serving hopes of course failed to materialize; instead the expected accommodations were only partially realized, and then only in an unscheduled, piecemeal fashion. In any case, new political classes that acceded to power tended to move African systems away from guided devolution toward less predictable, less manageable national politics. It is in the rise and triumph of these new groups and individuals—in opposition to the Anglicized colonial bourgeoisie who were schooled to be the heirs of the colonial system—that yet another context for the growth of political corruption can be found.

---

neglects the appearances of prosperity—be he chief, official, or politician—is likely to be more frequently criticized for his stinginess than praised for his austerity. "One of the primary uses of money in Ghanaian society," notes Maxwell Owusu, "is its consumption and distribution to acquire high social status and prestige." *Uses and Abuses of Power* (Chicago: University of Chicago Press, 1971), p. 91. Another colleague has raised a question that I have not been able to answer satisfactorily: "When does conspicuous consumption, or political corruption, by leaders become intolerable to followers?" How, or why, or when does the cathartic consumption of yesterday become today's loathsome excess? The query focuses on the old problem of the threshold of legitimacy—the point at which followers have "had enough" of their leaders. I admit I do not know. It probably varies with time, place, and circumstance. My best guess is that the threshold is crossed when most followers agree that their leader(s) no longer deliver(s) political goods according to their expectations, be those goods symbolic, intangible, or material.

The social and educational character of Ghana's "new men" is well summarized by F. K. Drah:

> Not long after World War II, many of the inter-war colonial movements spearheaded by moderate leaders, were overwhelmed by the radical, militant nationalist movements of the "new men." The change in the leadership of the nationalist movement in Ghana was much more profound than elsewhere in British West Africa.
>
> The "young men" of Ghana comprised about four types of people. First, there was the politically half-articulate section of the illiterate "commoner" people in the local authority chiefdoms. Secondly, there was the growing number of semi-illiterate, discontented younger elements who had just arrived in the urban areas from the rural hinterlands. The small, but quite obstreperous and status-conscious number of journalists, elementary school teachers and ex-servicemen formed a third group. Finally there was the steadily mounting number of commercial and semi-industrial workers who found themselves excluded from the competition for the urban status, but were all too clearly aware of the role they could play in the post-war "climate of economic development." The last three groups were largely composed of elementary-school-leavers, the proverbial "Standard VII boys." It was people representing a cross section of these "young men," together with the political phenomenon that was Kwame Nkrumah, "the show boy," who cleverly captured the leadership of the nationalist movement from such stalwarts as Dr. Danquah and his colleagues.[19]

This group is difficult to define, not only because of its heterogenous social composition, but because it included not only those mentioned by Drah, but also clerks and messengers in government and commercial offices, petty traders and storekeepers, artisans and taxi and truck drivers, as well as small-scale contractors and businessmen. Its members are probably best described as "transclass men," to use Ali Mazrui's term.[20] They hovered between town and countryside, only partially detached from their villages, operating at the social and economic margins of the larger towns that on the whole tended to be dominated by members of the well established colonial middle class: intellectuals, professionals, administrative auxiliaries of the colonial regime, and "old families" whose members had long ago made peace with the British through commercial, social, or political channels. Jitendra Mohan uses the term "petty bourgeoisie" to label the new group; this may be a somewhat strained use of the term, but it does help to distinguish them from the colonial elite, which was itself an alliance of the colonial middle class and those traditional magnates who had accommodated themselves to the colonial fact.[21] Whatever the proper label—"transclass," "new men," "petty bourgeoisie," "youngmen,"—this group inherited the Ghanaian political kingdom in 1951, and its leaders brought to government attitudes, values, and a political style that owed little to the political norms espoused by either the British or the colonial elite.

As a group, the leaders who organized the CPP and won the crucial 1951 parliamentary elections mirrored their constituents. With some notable exceptions, they were politically inexperienced, gullible, impatient, and almost revolutionary in outlook. Their self-revealing slogan, "Self-government Now!" stood in sharp contrast to the more accommodationist, gradualist attitude that guided the United Gold Coast Convention led by members of the colonial elite. "Politics in the pre-CPP era," writes Mohan, "was altogether a quiet and dignified affair.... Politics in the CPP era was by contrast a noisy and hectic affair; it was the politics of the market-place and the election platform"[22] The "youngmen," according to Austin and Drah, gained their experience of authority and power under colonial rule as "commoners" within the local authority chiefdoms, "and it was in their very nature as 'commoners' not to have recognized the faint traces of liberalism within colonial rule. They saw and experienced only its despotic aspects."[23] The political vision Nkrumah held before them, on the other hand, promised not only the seemingly limitless powers and prerogatives enjoyed by the British and the colonial elite, but their own rapid accession to the attendant status and privileges. They were men socialized to one of the important consequences of colonialism—what Owusu called the "economization" of politics; thus it is hardly surprising that when political resources fell to their control they regarded them in highly personal, instrumental terms, and the restraining bureaucratic norms of the colonial elite, as well as the older traditional curbs on the abuse of office, held little operative meaning for them. Moreover, the narrow social distance between them and their constituents made them seek artificial distinctions to widen the gap. In the process, the leaders of this "transclass" were caught up in what Mazrui calls "the quest for aristocratic effect," a form of social ostentation that was manifested in splendid attire, large and expensive cars, palatial living accommodations, and other forms of conspicuous consumption. At the very top, this quest fostered a "monarchical tendency"; elsewhere, at least at the elite levels, it meant the widespread use of public political resources for the acquisition and distribution of visible, ego-inflating private and public goods.[24]

When Ghana became independent in 1957, the "new men" were firmly in control. They had managed to overcome the only serious challenge to their power launched by the old coalition, the so-called federalist agitation of 1954–56; they had successfully laid a financial substructure for the CPP by gaining control of cocoa purchasing and the funds of the Cocoa Marketing Board; they had created a single-party system that "served to produce out of the petty bourgeoisie mass a substantial bureaucratic bourgeoisie entrenched in the state apparatus at all levels.[25]

The 1960–61 changes in the party as highlighted by Nkrumah's "Dawn Broadcast" were made largely, as we noted previously, in an attempt to undermine the political standing of the Party "old guard." They failed to affect the basic character of the elite since their main consequence was simply to replace one venal group with another. Again, Mohan's judgment is harsh, but accurate:

> The new party structure was . . . simply a heap of career openings which were stuffed with persons without political experience or popular credentials but endowed with an unusual capacity for singing Nkrumah's praises. Those persons were all too willingly drawn into the CPP's dominant ethos of self-seeking, careerism and corruption. They became critics of the party's "old guard"—the bureaucratic bourgeoisie—in the hope of displacing the latter from the state apparatus and of inheriting its economic rewards.[26]

The post-Kulungugu "counterrevolution" of 1962–63 brought yet another round of musical chairs, with the Party's "old guard" once again coming out on top. With variations, this game continued until February 1966.

In sum, the "new men," because of their background, their outlook, and the manner in which they rose to power, became at once a fertile field for the cultivation of political corruption and willing co-workers in that cultivation. All this is not to imply that the colonial bourgeoisie would have behaved any better had they inherited power, as they and the British had planned. There is no way of knowing, since they never got the chance. Not even the character of the Busia regime (1969–72), an interesting amalgam of surviving members of the colonial bourgeoisie and "new men" who fell out with Nkrumah at one point or another, permits such speculation. But if contexts for the development of political corruption in Ghana are sought, the "new men" in or out of power must be considered prime candidates. They did not, of course, "cause" political corruption; they did become major propagators.

Bureaucratic Transitions and Growth of Corruption

Virtually every country that has recently become independent appears, at least initially, to have undergone a great expansion of governmental activity accompanied by a proliferation of official agencies and functions. Ghana is no exception. From 1951 to 1961 the proportion of government employees to the total number of wage earners in the country rose from 43 percent to 61 percent; by 1960 some 189,990 persons were employed in the public sector, or 19,494 more than in 1959 and nearly two and one-half times the 1950 figure.[27] An even greater increase is registered in recurrent expenditures of the central government: for 1950–51 the figure was about $39 million; by fiscal 1961–62 it had risen to about $228 million, of which approximately 53 percent could be attributed to the costs of personnel administration (salaries, offices, perquisites, pensions, etc.)[28] These figures are hardly unusual; they reflect a pattern common to new nations, and in fact budgets 65 percent devoted to administrative costs are not uncommon in African countries. More unusual, however—even unique in Africa—is the spectacular growth of the structures of government in Ghana as a consequence of the socialist statism of the Nkrumah regime. Before independence, even with the new postwar structures of ministries, boards, legislatures, and the like, the institutions of Gold Coast government were relatively modest in size and scope. By 1965, however, according to Elliot J. Berg, Ghana had become an "administrative jungle":

> There were thirty-one ministries. Statutory corporations were scattered all over the place. It is not certain that at any one time anybody knew

just how many there were. Key operating ministries were cut up periodically, their functions divided, then shuttled back and forth. Agriculture was the best example: between the old ministry, the State Farms Corporation, the United Ghana Farmers' Council, the Agricultural Wing of the Workers' Brigade, and twenty-five other agencies, lines of authority were hopelessly tangled, coordination inexistent, and personal access to political figures more important in decisions than technical or economic issues.[29]

What Berg is describing is the state system in full flower with political corruption flourishing at all levels. His "jungle" metaphor is apt not only because it suggests almost unrestrained institutional growth, but because it evokes a sense of the difficulties attending political life during the First Republic. For the elite inhabitants of Berg's "jungle"—at least for the "new men"—survival depended in large measure on learning the rules by which Nkrumah, the party, and the rest of the elite played their zero-sum games, on building personal defenses (such as networks of reciprocal support involving family, tribe, clients, patrons, and subordinates) against the destructive winds of factional conflict, and on successfully manipulating both the values and the goods of the culture of political corruption. The metaphor also suggests another important context within which Ghanaian political corruption developed, a context whose principal elements are those outlined above: an unstable, highly fragmented administrative structure; a burgeoning but insecure officialdom; and increasing political resources made accessible to a regime whose program and goals were inconsistent and often contradictory. A summary look at the first two elements may help to illustrate their relationship to each other and to the growth of Ghanaian political corruption.

The Public Service. By all accounts, the colonial bureaucracy in Ghana compared favorably with similar public services elsewhere in Africa. It was staffed by expatriates and a small number of Ghanaians taken into the Colonial Service in the years just before and after World War II. Owing to the restrictions inherent in the recruitment process, the Ghanaians admitted to public service were men of exceptional merit who were also usually well-connected in Ghanaian society. They constituted an elite in the strictest sense of the word, and they tended to stamp the service with their image. They were jealous of its competence and status and constituted a bulwark against ill-considered change and the deterioration of standards. With few exceptions, they remained aloof from party politics except for the considerable role they played behind the scenes in the formulation of party and government policies.[30] In short, they were men steeped in the colonial tradition of law and order, and they tended to see the bureaucratic apparatus as an instrument for control rather than for development. Their political problems began with the enormous growth of the public service in the years just before and after independence, and with the accelerated demand for Africanization (simply, the replacement of expatriates by locals).

The conservatism of the establishment bureaucracy stood in sharp contrast to the dynamism of the "new men" bent on rapid transformation of the Ghanaian polity according to the socialist vision of the CPP leadership. That vision may have been somewhat blurred, but there was no denying either its timely appeal or the vigorous intent behind it. Hence it was almost inevitable that when expatriates vacated offices or when positions opened in new structures of government, the posts were rapidly filled by representatives of the new group. Ambitious and often badly trained, they predictably ran afoul of their colonial confrères for stylistic, professional, and ideological reasons. It was not long before the "new men" in national office began to protest what they deemed the obstructive tactics of the old bureaucracy and its failure to adopt attitudes supportive of the regime. The regime responded along four related lines: an attempt was made to politicize the bureaucracy, Africanization was turned to new directions, the party was given semi-supervisory powers vis-à-vis the bureaucracy, and the top positions in the proliferating administrative superstructure were increasingly filled by the politically faithful rather than by technicians or professional bureaucrats.

The civil service remained relatively free from party influence until 1961, when Nkrumah assumed control of the public services under provisions of the Republican constitution. The change, it must be admitted, did not come unheralded. On at least two previous occasions, Nkrumah had spoken of the need for a public service on whom the regime could count for unfailing support. On November 12, 1956, in a speech before the Legislative Assembly, he expressed strong hopes for a responsive, "representative" (but apolitical) post-independence civil service. On June 30, 1959, he issued a more pointed warning, in a speech which launched the Second Development Plan. That speech included an open declaration of war on recalcitrant and "disloyal" elements in the civil service:

> To all those civil servants who feel they cannot with a clear conscience give loyal service to the Government, my advice is that they should resign from the service at once. . . . It is our intention to tighten up the regulations and to wipe out the disloyal elements in the civil service . . . for disloyal civil servants are no better than saboteurs.[31]

There is no evidence that the service was actually disloyal to the regime, but as Robert Dowse points out, it had certainly kept aloof from the CPP and was clearly ill-disposed toward the upstarts who flooded the bureaucracy between 1951 and 1961. What is more, given its elite origins, it had difficulty sympathizing with the new petty-bourgeois leadership. In 1959 the senior civil service was partially purged with the dismissal of several key persons, including Robert Gardiner, the British-trained Ghanaian who headed the establishment Secretariat. Next, in June 1960, a College of Administration was set up to train CPP-oriented civil servants; and in 1961, as we have noted, the civil service was placed directly within the control of the Office of the President.[32] Throughout 1962 and 1963 the pressure on "bourgeois remnants" in the civil service was kept up by both the party and the leaders of the regime; the final act in the confrontation came in 1964 when, following approval of the constitutional amendment that made Ghana officially a one-party state, the party established planning bodies controlled by the President's Office which became, along with the Ghana Bank, the most critical administrative organs of the state.[33]

It should be added that even though the regime made every attempt to politicize the bureaucracy, it never formally integrated the party and the public service. Rather, according to Henry Bretton, Nkrumah actually encouraged the civil service—or at least its top-echelon members—to adopt a posture of independence from the party. Both party and civil service were to be kept on a leash held by the president, but the party was to be the watchdog over the public service. At the same time, Nkrumah expanded the party bureaucracy and shook it up periodically, but allowed it little operational power below the District Commissioner level. It was to be but one of the political groups in Ghana—albeit the largest and most overlapping and hence conflicting, with none permitted to develop independent power.[34] In sum, a situation was created that maximized official insecurity, and in this ambiance more often than not officials in both the party and the public services felt driven to illicit and informal measures, if only to protect themselves and their jobs.

The personal insecurity of officials was further aggravated by the course of "Ghanaization" (Ghana's version of Africanization) in the public service. Initially, the purposes and procedures of this policy were relatively straightforward: it was designed to phase out British Colonial Service officials wherever they could be replaced by qualified Ghanaians, and to increase the percentage of Ghanaians at the top echelons in areas of the civil service in which overseas officers were still needed. In both respects, the program appeared to be a marked success. For example, between 1949 and 1954 the percentage of Ghanaians holding Senior Officer grades in the public service rose from 13.8 percent to 38.2 percent,[35] and by 1961 Ghanaians comprised nearly 80 percent of the senior ranks.

These figures, however, conceal the fact that there was a rise in the absolute number of expatriates in Ghana's senior public service between 1949 and 1965: 1,068 in 1949, 1,490 in 1954, and no fewer than 1,900 by 1965 (according to Berg, there were 800 expatriates in the civil service in 1965, of whom more than 500 were teachers; another 600 were employed in state enterprises, and about 500 were technical-assistance experts[36]). At the time of independence, the number of British civil servants in Ghana had actually declined somewhat from preceding years; the rising expatriate figures since then is attributable chiefly to the subsequent arrival of large numbers of non-British personnel, including Russians, Poles, Czechs, Yugoslavs, Italians, and Americans, as well as U.N. personnel from a half-dozen countries. What is more, military personnel from the Soviet Union and China were brought in to help train African "liberation fighters" at several secret camps around the country, and although they were not included in the official figures their numbers were felt. Hence by the mid-sixties it appeared to many Ghanaian public servants that the net effect of Ghanaization had been to cede the managerial and technical heights of the economy and the administration to foreigners. Certainly, the presence in their midst of hundreds of expatriates who owed their jobs to the Presidency and who often literally spoke a different language, could only undermine the Ghanaians' sense of efficacy and increase their sense of job insecurity.

Structural Fragmentation We return now to the situation that inspired Berg's "jungle" metaphor. By 1965 Ghana had become an almost classic example of an administrative system on the verge of breakdown:[37] a proliferation of agencies was accompanied by a shortage of trained personnel to man the newly created positions, administrative shortcutting had contributed greatly to a decline in coordination and communication within the public sector, the decision-making process was erratic and disorderly, budget capacity and financial control were deteriorating, and the civil service was insecure and rent by internal conflict.

The proliferation of governmental structures began, as we noted, in the ambitious plans of a statist regime to mobilize the country's material and human resources with maximal speed. Berg argues that it also owed something to the conflict in the civil service between the "new men" in office and the older public servants who were thought to be both unenthusiastic and recalcitrant about putting the new programs into effect. For these reasons, and also perhaps because of the inability of existing administrative agencies to cope with increased requirements, the political leadership elected to try various structural short cuts, and to set up new and hopefully more responsive administrative units.

One result [according to Berg] is that administrative coordination, never well developed to begin with, becomes immensely more difficult. Procedures for decision-making take on an increasingly ad hoc character. Available trained and experienced people are spread over more administrative units, increasing the need for coordination while the capacity to coordinate declines. The incentive to coordinate also declines. When the system loosens to the point where ministries and a large variety of state corporations and agencies are able to make budget and foreign aid commitments without much screening and control at the center, everything goes up for grabs. Any ministry that doesn't do as its less finicky public sector counterparts are doing will fall behind in budget allocations, in personnel, in status. Under the worst assumptions about motivation, there are pockets to be lined by these activities. Under more benign assumptions, each minister or statutory corporation head identifies his task with the forward progress and welfare of the country.[38]

Under any assumption, the results were the same: uncontrolled expenditures, free-wheeling state enterprises, and an entrepreneurial ethic that permitted wholesale trade in public resources. In addition, this fragmentation of the administrative system gave easy entry to a variety of outside promoters, salesmen, and brokers who offered a dazzling array of "supplier credits," equipment, projects, and benefits to enhance the status of an agency or line the pockets of its managers.[39]

The regime had always aspired to a tightly organized, well-oiled, centralized government machine able to rapidly transform the economy and the society; what it eventually got was exactly the opposite. It also got political corruption on a massive scale, with virtually everyone in a position to take advantage of it, including the President, in on the take.

Unfortunately, the fragmentation of the administrative system, together with at least some of its attendant problems, persisted into the post-Nkrumah era. The extent and magnitude of political corruption diminished somewhat, to be sure, in the wake of reforms undertaken by both the NLC and Busia regimes. However, one other aspect of the situation remained substantially unchanged: the old relationship between administrative fragmentation on the one hand and bureaucratic density, inter-office articulation, and political corruption on the other. In less formal terms, that relationship can be described as follows: in a fragmented administrative system, the greater the concentration of officials in one general locale (i.e., the greater the bureaucratic density), the less likely they are to coordinate (i.e., to articulate) their activities, and the more likely they are to engage in acts of political corruption.

The author observed this phenomenon at first hand during the years 1969–71, when he lived and worked near Accra, the administrative center of Ghana, and had repeated opportunities to visit many of the state-run offices, ministries, boards, and enterprises headquartered in that city. He was repeatedly struck by the large numbers of persons employed in these agencies, and indeed was told that about 65 percent of the country's bureaucrats were concentrated in Accra. A casual walk through the Ministry of Information building in 1970, for example, revealed some 460 people at least nominally on the job. This ministry functioned mainly to produce and distribute various reports and documents concerning the government's activities. Yet it proved extremely difficult to find anyone there who could say what had been published, much less find the published materials, and in general, a purchase of documents could not be concluded in less than an hour. In course of a visit to the Ministry of Trade for an export license (to ship the family dog home) the author called at eight offices, contacted at least a dozen officials, and consumed the better part of a morning. The business of clearing goods from the Tema Harbor at that time normally took anywhere from four days to a month because the numerous persons who must supply all the requisite signatures, seals, approvals, and papers were never on hand at one time, and those encountered at any step along the way were likely to be completely unaware of the next step in the process. Similar frustrations were met at the ministries of Interior, Agriculture, and Finance. Withal, the dominant impression to be gained was that people in one office were extraordinarily insulated from those in other offices, and no one seemed to be willing to provide any service not specifically related to his own office or job description. When the time came for the author to leave Ghana, it required no less than twenty-six trips to Accra, fifty-five pieces of official paper, contact with at least eighty-seven officials, and about thirteen full working days to complete all the formalities and secure all the necessary clearances for departure. The author was told his experience was not unusual; part of the problem, he was told, was his failure to offer the usual "gifts" and bribes and, worse, his unwillingness to comply when on at least nine occasions he was directly asked for some sort of "favour," "gift," or "dash" in exchange for a service, a signature, or an official stamp. Lest it be thought that these difficulties confronted only expatriates, conversations with Ghanaian friends and articles in Accra newspapers indicated that Ghanaians without "pull" had an even worse time of it.

These observations are admittedly somewhat unsystematic, but they serve to add dimension to the picture of administrative fragmentation. The attitudes they express are probably in large part a legacy of the Nkrumah era and its uncertainties, which fostered the view that an official position was a *situation acquise* to be defended against all comers and fortified by networks of supportive relationships. The same conditioned awareness made office-holders hypersensitive to jurisdictional lines (lest other office-holders feel threatened by intrusion), and thus they cultivated a calculated ignorance of what went on in anyone else's official domain. One of the net results was that decisions, even unimportant ones, tended to be pushed on the men at the top (the author finally got his export license, incidentally, when he accidentally walked into the Ministerial Secretary's office). Furthermore, as the number of offices and officials at all levels increased and were packed into Accra, the old insecurities increased and with them, the tendencies to dis-articulation. Thus administrative fragmentation became in a sense a self-fulfilling prophecy, not only as between agencies, but very often *within* them. And one of the important consequences of the growing dis-articulation (and its concomitant loss of control) was that the opportunities for political corruption increased enormously: merely to function at all, if for no other reason, office-holders became individual political entrepreneurs, each at his own level operating according to whatever personal techniques he could develop and whatever political resources he could control.

The Consequences of Political Corruption

The vigorous debate between those who argue the "toxic" vs. the "tonic" effects of political corruption has been admirably summarized by Professor Heidenheimer, and we shall not repeat it here.[40] That debate cannot be definitively resolved for the simple reason that on both sides the arguments are persuasive on the basis of the evidence presented. At the risk of seeming naïve, one might say it all boils down to the proposition that corruption is sometimes tonic and sometimes toxic, depending on how political corruption is defined, what are the particularities of the situation under study, and what are deemed the requisites of political or economic development. We do not wish to imply that these analyses are inconsequential; they have in fact generated useful hypotheses about the incidence of corruption, the conditions for its growth, and some of its more tangible effects, and as the preceding pages testify, our analysis has benefited considerably from these contributions.

Before entering our own argument about consequences in the lists, a few words are necessary about what is possibly the most sophisticated of recent attempts to assess the probable effects of corruption on political development, Joseph S. Nye's "Cost-Benefit Analysis."[41] That analysis provides a scheme that might be useful in comparative analysis, and thus might have implications for our study of Ghana.[42]

Nye presents a matrix which lists a number of national development problems together with various types of corruption. Political development is defined in terms of political legitimacy; hence, according to Nye, in order to maintain legitimacy a regime must be able to cope in three major spheres: it must foster economic development, it must push national integration, and it must increase governmental capacity to cope with social change. Corruption may serve these ends and thus benefit a society when the public and such key groups as the army have a generally tolerant attitude toward corruption, when the political elite feel secure enough to invest their capital at home rather than send it to Swiss banks, and when restraints on corruption exist in the form of an independent press, opposition parties, trade unions, or fair elections. Positing the conditions cited, Nye concludes that corruption may (a) enhance economic development (by stimulating capital formation, bureaucratic efficiency, and the creation of entrepreneurs and entrepreneurial incentive); (b) speed national integration (by fostering inter-elite coordination and supportive, participatory attitudes among rural non-elites); and (c) increase governmental capacity (through the development of greater effectiveness and legitimacy). Nye also lists a number of possible costs, but the burden of his argument is clearly on the side of the proposition that—as Heidenheimer puts it—"a smattering of corruption may help keep the masses politically satisfied"[43] and aid developmental efforts.

Obviously, Nye's scheme is not fully applicable to our analysis. Only one of his three benefit conditions—the first condition—applies to Ghana, and that only partially. What we have called the "culture of political corruption" may have predisposed most Ghanaians to tolerate a certain amount of corruption, but that toleration may have been more a function of resignation than of acquiescence, and in any case the fact that all post-independence Ghanaian governments —including Nkrumah's—have evinced much concern about the problem shows they have perceived limits to the public's tolerance. Further, if our assessment of the traditional contexts of corruption is correct, the Ghanaian norms for judging corruption must have retarded the growth of public tolerance. To be sure, these involved in corruption (see chapter 3) have shown high tolerance for it, but even they do not often argue that it is beneficial to either the government or the economy.

The second condition in Nye's scheme does not generally apply.

Ghana's ruling elite could not be described as "secure" at any time except perhaps in the days immediately before and after independence. There is evidence that at least some of the capital derived from corruption was invested outside the country and indeed that some of it did go to Swiss banks; more commonly, however, it appears to have been spent on conspicuous consumption. Even when members of the elite invested their gains in business at home, as many did, it is doubtful that their activities had much positive impact on the Ghanaian economic system. The pattern revealed by our study indicates there was little "trickling down" benefit to the public at large either from the elite's own private investments or from much of its use of public resources for economic and social development.

Nye's condition regarding institutional restraints on corruption applies even less to Ghana. The country has never enjoyed a free and independent press. During much of the Nkrumah period there was virtually no independent press; during the NLC years there was a murmur of press criticism, but it was short lived; and during the Busia regime only one or two fitful voices, such as that of *The Spokesman*, were raised in dissent, and they were often subjected to official persecution. Opposition parties, such as they were, were unable to exercise much restraining influence. Their members in parliament frequently denounced the excesses of government during both the Nkrumah and Busia regimes, to be sure, but with negligible effect. Trade unions on occasion demonstrated both independence and opposition to Ghanaian government; however, they were usually more concerned about basic economic issues, such as poor pay in the face of rising costs of living, than about official corruption. Finally, after 1957 "fair elections" were held too infrequently to exercise much restraint on corruption. Only during the elections of 1969, which brought the Busia government to power, did past corruption (during the Nkrumah regime) become something of a campaign issue.

If Nye's conditions cannot be met satisfactorily for Ghana, the probabilities that the benefits of Ghanaian corruption outweighed the costs obviously decline sharply. It remains, then, to try to assess the costs of Ghanaian corruption assuming they outweigh the benefits. Here it becomes extremely difficult, if not impossible, to apply a Nye-style analysis to Ghana. Nye's matrix anticipates only two situations in which costs would outweigh benefits, and both require *favorable* political conditions—i.e., cultural tolerance, elite security, checks on corruption.[44] As we have seen, these conditions do not apply in the case of Ghana (and it should be noted that they do not apply in most African cases). Moreover, Nye's conclusion that a "smattering of corruption" may be functional to development (a point of view shared by a good many analysts of corruption) rests on the implied assumptions that (1) it is somehow possible to determine how much corruption is beneficial, and that (2) government will be able to limit the scale of corruption, if not its incidence. Neither assumption seems justified by the evidence gleaned in this study: we do not know at what point functional corruption becomes dysfunctional (gross, large-scale losses excepted), and it appears that once political corruption has taken root it tends to grow rapidly unless checked by stern or, ultimately, draconian methods. The regimes among the developing nations that have succeeded in substantially curbing political corruption have been very few in number (indeed, only two recent examples come to mind—the People's Republic of China and the government of Prime Minister Lee Kuan Yew of Singapore). Ghana cannot yet be counted among that number.[45]

But if Nye's analysis is of little help in the Ghanaian case in *assessing* either benefits or costs of corruption, it still provides useful categories for our discussion of consequences. On the debit side of the cost-benefit ledger, Nye lists three broad rubrics: waste of resources, instability, and reduction of governmental capacity.[46] We shall consider each in turn.

Waste of Resources   Nye argues that corruption may contribute to an economically damaging waste of resources in four ways: by causing a capital outflow (to Swiss banks, for example) resulting in a net loss to the economy; by fostering projects ostensibly designed to be economically profitable but actually designed to conceal diversion of capital to corrupt fees or procurement of cost-plus contracts and suppliers' credits; by directing available skills to corrupt enrichment rather than to productive enterprise; and by discouraging foreign aid from donors reluctant to see their aid misused.

Of the four possibilities, the second most closely describes the visible situation in Ghana during the Nkrumah period. Even one of the most charitable commentators on Ghana's economy between 1957 and 1965, Reginald Green, condemned what he saw as "utterly implausible ventures," "ineffective or irrational implementation," "unselective and untested importation of large-scale mechanized techniques," "inadequate public sector management," "misuse of funds and incompetence in high places," and the like.[47] For example, the operations of the State Farms Corporation for the 27-month period ended December 31, 1965, cost $21 million (including $10 million for wages and salaries) while the value of corporate production in that period was only $4 million; this left a deficit of $17 million. Frequently, investment policies in some sectors were not based on sound economic considerations. Jon Woronoff comments:

> The most costly mistakes were made at the highest levels. Rather than select plants to meet known needs, they were acquired rather haphazardly by politicians, ministers, and the President. Each junket to the East brought new purchases, and the less scrupulous Western businessmen sold projects through their contacts in the party. Thus the factories were not only expensive, they were sometimes obsolete or unusable. Above all, they were too big and numerous. One of the first factories to go up was the Kwame Nkrumah Steel Works in Tema, which used scrap iron to manufacture steel pipe. The building and machinery were imposing, so much so that the works ran at about one-third capacity; but it produced a size pipe that unfortunately was not in use in Ghana. The shoe factory in Kumasi was oversized and largely automated, the shoes it produced were sturdy and elegant, but a bit warm for the tropics and far more expensive than the locally-made sandals. And it was hard to understand why Ghana decided to build an atomic reactor.[48]

Other examples of disastrous investment abound. For example, of about $40 million worth of tractors purchased from Yugoslavia and Czechoslovakia, 80 percent became inoperable after a short period of time; the Asutuare sugar scheme was started in an area without proper soils or adequate water; the Accra-Tema Motorway, a four-lane divided highway built at a cost of $11 million, was but eighteen miles long and only marginally useful; the secret $18 million Bolgatanga airport project was never completed, despite virtually unlimited financing and help from abroad; some 60 earth-fill catchment dams, in all costing over $5 million were for the most part either unnecessary or silted up within two years; and, of course, the imposing "Job 600" complex, a major convention complex costing over $30 million, was built to serve a single meeting of the Organization of African Unity in 1965. (The huge twelve-story main building of "Job 600" consisted of some 60 separate suites, each with its own elevator and with kitchens, baths, bedrooms, living rooms, etc., to accommodate one full national delegation; moreover each suite was equipped with listening devices so Nkrumah could monitor his guests' conversations.) Many similar instances of ill-conceived expenditure have already been noted in this study, and many more could be listed.

In addition, Nye's first, third, and fourth possibilities apply to Ghana, though with what force, and at what cost it is impossible to know. How much went into Swiss banks, for example, is a mystery; the author heard varying figures ranging from $3 million to $30 million.

Withal, the basic question remains unanswered as to how much of Ghana's wasted resources resulted from political corruption. The data suggest a heavy toll, but in the absence of detailed, comprehensive accounting and some reasonably accurate way of separating losses due to corruption from those owing to other factors such as mis-management and imcompetence, no dollars-and-cents estimate can be given. While we can give no figure, however, the existence of widespread political corruption has been established beyond doubt, and it is clear that corrupt practices hampered the function of a variety of public enterprises and sabotaged not a few investment opportunities.

Instability Nye argues that insofar as corruption destroys the legitimacy of political structures in the eyes of those who have power to do something about the situation, it contributes to instability and might possibly lead to national disintegration. Again, there are no empirical indices to establish a reliable measure of the relationship, if any, between corruption and Ghana's two coups d'etat. Yet it can be argued that corruption contributed to the aura of disillusion that preceded the coups of 1966 and 1972 and made it impossible for either the Nkrumah regime or the Busia regime to find popular (or elite) support when the chips were down.

It may well be that political corruption has certain salutary short-range benefits for a developing system—for example, by bypassing immobile or clogged bureaucratic channels, redistributing political goods more widely than does the official system, and fostering both political and commercial entrepreneurship. In the long run, however, it is hard to see how such benefits can remain benefits given the growth proclivity of politically corrupt networks, the tendency for corrupt behavior to become ever more extensive within the system, and the virtual impossibility of limiting wastage of political resources by edict, prosecution, or exposure. One of the most important functions of government is to provide goods and services to qualified recipients on a regular, *predictable* basis. Goods and services allocated through politically corrupt transactions have two important drawbacks: they tend to be distributed on a highly selective basis (to persons in informal networks), and their distribution tends to be unreliable because the goods themselves are closely tied to the political fortunes and position of the distributor/office-holder. Individuals who are not tied into one of the distributive networks get left out altogether or at best (assuming some of the benefits "dribble down"), are less favored than their neighbors who have inside connections. From this it is easy to see how in a political system in which the culture of political corruption has taken root the allocation of political goods engenders social inequalities and accentuates those that already exist. In Ghana, the gap between the haves and the have-nots—one of the ills specifically targeted for correction under socialism— in fact increased during the Nkrumah era, with the lot of the urban unemployed, the marginal farmer, the peasant, and the ethnically out of favor[49] becoming worse rather than better. Such people do not make enthusiastic supporters of a regime. Further, as the distribution of political goods becomes increasingly unreliable or idiosyncratic, political fealty becomes progressively atomized, accreting to individuals and groups in favorable distributive positions rather than to the regime or its institutions.

The net long-run effect is a loss of legitimacy for the regime and an unwillingness on the part of citizens to be mobilized to great ends. Nkrumah's "Dawn Broadcast" was privately derided by his colleagues and received with cynicism by the public because the corruption of the regime was by then already too patent to be concealed. Similarly, Prime Minister Busia's call for "discipline" and self-denial, and the gesture by which he and his ministers cut their own salaries, were greeted with general disbelief, particularly since the same leaders refused to reveal their assets (as required by the Constitution) and took few pains to conceal their high style of living.

Reduction of Government Capacity In our earlier discussions we have seen how corruption contributes to structural fragmentation and exacerbates problems of bureaucratic transition, thus reducing government capacity to cope with the challenges it must confront. As Nye points out, a loss of governmental capacity is another major factor that engenders loss of legitimacy. Any loss of legitimacy is of course perilous—and if a regime loses its legitimacy in the eyes of a politically important group, such as the young Army officers, the consequences can be disastrous.

Finally, the reduction of governmental capacity is the more serious in newly independent countries because their governments carry a greater burden of popular expectation than older regimes. The coming of independence is often accompanied by almost millenial expectations, and the fact that those who accede to power have usually played a role in stirring up these expectations in no way abates the effect. The governments of new states are expected to provide prompt solutions to social problems that may have resisted earnest attempts at remedy for generations, to achieve advanced economic development overnight where there was perhaps none before, and to deliver a wide variety of symbolic and material goods that may never even have been expected of the colonial power.

Thus any regime in a newly independent country is hard put to reconcile its goals and programs with public demand on the one hand and hard necessity on the other. If, like the Ghanaian regime, it falls far short of its goals and at the same time dissipates scarce resources in wholesale political corruption, it can only decrease its chances of political survival.

— 6 —

Ghanaian Political Corruption
in Perspective

Throughout this study, an attempt has been made to lend perspective to Ghanaian political corruption by alluding to similar circumstances in other countries. It may now be useful to review some of these observations and in addition to emphasize some of the differences between political corruption in Ghana and political corruption elsewhere, particularly in the industrialized states of Europe and North America. The two major themes of Chapter 5—the consequences and causes of political corruption—seem particularly useful points of reference for this purpose, and they are the focus of this discussion.

The extent and ramifications of political corruption in the United States and various European countries are sufficiently well known to need little additional comment here, and in large measure our analysis of the corruption process applies as readily to them as to Ghana and to other polities in Africa, Asia, and Latin America. The use of large campaign contributions as a means of obligating candidates to donors or to special interests has long been an unfortunate feature of political life in the United States, and various kinds of electoral frauds—from ballot stuffing to vote-buying—have regularly been practiced on both sides of the Atlantic. The Aranda revelations in France during 1972, the German political scandals of 1973, and the extraordinary greed displayed by a series of military and civilian governments in Indochina over the past twenty years (for example), serve as reminders of the persistence and worldwide incidence of the phenomenon.* But there is an important difference between political

---

* I do not here include the sexual exploits of Messrs. Profumo, Lambton, and Jellicoe and their attendant political embarrassment to the British government, mainly because the exchange of official favors

corruption in the United States and other highly industrialized states and corruption in Ghana, Indonesia, Nigeria, and other third world countries. To put it baldly, poor countries can much less afford the political and economic costs of corruption than rich countries.[1]

Obviously, in a country where economic resources are scarce, the dissipation or misappropriation of, say, $100 million has a much greater effect on the economy than does the wastage of a like sum in a richer country. But beyond that, if one could compute equivalent amounts and imagine that, for example, 10 percent of the total resources is wasted in each of two given economies—one rich and highly industrialized, one poor and underdeveloped—the poorer economy will still be harder hit than the richer one. The economic impact—and hence the political impact—of *any wastage at all* is greater in the poorer country. This is so because that country's unmet needs will be much greater while the resources it has available for redistribution (to compensate for wastage) will be much smaller, or may in fact be nonexistent.

Thus in Africa, where most political and economic systems operate on the margins of viability, misuse of governmental resources can easily have results that are politically and economically disastrous. And as the examples of Ghana, Western Nigeria, and pre-1966 Upper Volta well attest, when a major medium of misuse is widespread political corruption, the chances of a disastrous outcome are greatly increased. We have seen how the blatant corruption practiced at all levels of the Nkrumah government after 1962 contributed in no small measure to its downfall and to the high degree of legitimacy accorded its military successors. The evidence is also strong that the Busia regime had lost much of its support by mid-1971 precisely because its leaders had begun to indulge in conspicuous consumption and open

---

between these ministers and the call girls involved only the diversion of what could at best be termed marginal public resources. Nor do I include instances of what was earlier called "corruption of the political process," though both kinds of activity, particularly the latter, can have as deleterious effect on the polity as the worst political corruption. Moreover, as was noted earlier, it is clear that "corruption of the political process" may well lead to political corruption, and vice versa. The 1970s Watergate affair in the United States is certainly testimony to this relationship.

trading in public goods similar to that practiced during the latter years of the Nkrumah regime.[2] And in the case of Western Nigeria there is solid evidence that the deterioration of political conditions after 1963 was significantly abetted by the activities of "kleptocrats" (Andreski's apt term for thieves in public office).[3]

A political system so affected need not, of course, collapse; there are other forms of political and economic disaster. It might become locked into either economic or political stagnation, or both. In that case, the unfortunate poor are usually condemned to continued misery, while the rulers bend their efforts chiefly to survival—often to a survival fraught with peril and uncertainty. In fact some of the better examples of politically corrupt systems—Haiti, Nicaragua, Honduras, Morocco—illustrate how such regimes might survive for some time. The case of Morocco makes the point most clearly. According to John Waterbury,

> Very few Moroccans have any illusions about the game: certainly not the King or the participants, nor, for the most part, the masses. . . . There is a general level of cynicism running throughout—the cynicism of the non-participating masses who fall back on the traditional reflex, "government has ever been thus"; the cynicism of the participants who partake of the system by refusing any responsibility for it; and the cynicism of the King who plays on the weakness and greed of his subjects. In this system, corruption serves only one "positive" function—that of survival of the regime. Resources are absorbed in patronage and are drained away from rational productive investment. Morocco remains fixed in a system of scarcity in which the vulnerable seek protection and thus regenerate the links of dependency and patronage that perpetuate the system. The dilemma for the ruler in such a system is whether, in the short term, his survival can be made compatible with rational administration and economic development, or whether, in the long term, it can be made compatible with planned corruption.[4]

Substitute "Ghanaians" and "Ghana" for "Moroccans" and "Morocco", "Nkrumah" and "the President" for "the King" and "the ruler," and the Moroccan case becomes almost indistinguishable from the Ghanaian situation between 1957 and 1966. The Ghanaian system, of course, simply collapsed in 1966 rather than lapsing into a protracted political and economic coma, perhaps because it had greater resilience and a somewhat different political tradition than Morocco, but the dilemma suggested above was no less real to Ghana's rulers while it lasted. (And as for Morocco, no reputable authority displays much confidence in the long-term prospects of the present regime.[5])

Corruption in poor countries also tends to differ from that of rich countries in its ubiquity. Unfortunately, in poorer countries politically corrupt practices often become standard operating procedure all up and down the ranks of officialdom, and what we have called the "culture of political corruption" tends to develop in a relatively short time. The "dash" that in Ghana became the conventional lubricant of transactions involving even the most modestly placed public servants—the constable on the roadblock, the postal clerk, the dispensary assistant, the junior clerk passing out forms—was one symptom of this tendency. In such situations, the public quickly learns to accept corrupt dealings with officials as one of the ordinary (and even inevitable) prices that must be paid for public services. And again, where public resources are scarce or limited their price tends to be high, particularly as they are dispensed in a pattern of corrupt practices.

Some of the Ghanaian contexts of corruption examined in chapter 5—administrative confusion and inefficiency, a norm structure that encourages self-seeking behavior, reinterpretation and redirection of traditional practices for the benefit of the new rulers, a lack of workable restraints, the insecurity and irresponsibility of the nation's top leaders—apply as well to other poor countries in Africa, Asia, and Latin America in far greater measure than they apply in most richer countries. To that complex of situations others can be added: patrimonial relations that tend to personalize rather than depersonalize political transactions, a wage structure that encourages extracurricular supplementation, inadequate training of officials, and the "demonstration effect" that permits corrupt practices at all levels on the excuse that "the others are doing it too." These circumstances, as we have seen, were present in Ghana and are also common in other poorer countries. Finally, the overriding causal nexus that supports and reinforces all the others is the fact of the relative poverty of the countries concerned. It is a point worth stressing again: in poorer countries, where political and economic goods are scarce and the demand for them increases as expectations of a better life rise, the price for the goods tends also to rise. And unless restrained in some way, those persons who can most readily pay the price—by definition, those most powerful—will effect a redistribution to their own benefit, be it through the instruments of government or through informal mechanisms like those described in these pages. Under these circumstances, officials in relatively modest positions tend to identify with the ruling elite and avail themselves of whatever their own authority can bring them. If use of a market metaphor to make the last point can be criticized on theoretical grounds, it nonetheless responds realistically to what Maxwell Owusu termed the "economization" of political and social relations in Ghana—and in other poorer countries.

It must be emphasized that this analysis does not assert that all officials in Ghana and elsewhere in Africa are politically corrupt, or even that most of them are. Nor does it contend that Ghana affords a unique example of political depravity, for that is hardly the case. Rather the point is that in a good many African countries political corruption is sufficiently pervasive that the public expect their politicians and public servants to be generally dishonest.

Nor do we deny that some rich countries support a burden of political corruption of considerable magnitude. In Italy, for example, the 1973 Arezzo trials revealed a pattern of corrupt dealings by officials of the government tax-collection agency between 1949 and 1954 that involved literally thousands of millions of lire.[6] However, in Italy the margins for accommodation were sufficient to offset the economic and political costs implied in these figures without irreparable harm to the system, and thus the normal public services continued to be delivered with relative competence (except during strikes) and without additional charge to the public. Of crucial importance, too is the fact that in Italy and most other richer countries corrupt political activities tend to be the exception rather than the rule, and even when they are relatively widespread they do not usually affect the performance of lower-echelon public servants or severely undermine the expectation that public services will be more or less fairly delivered. One important difference, then, in the incidence and impact of political corruption as between rich and poor countries lies in the relative political and economic margins available to absorb the costs of corruption. In broader perspective, the poor-vs.-rich country dichotomy aside, differences in incidence and impact of corruption also probably relate to the presence or absence of such things as effective institutionalized checks against corruption, the diffusion of norms against self-seeking official behavior, and (in democratic polities) the kinds of structural constraints posited by Nye (active political opposition, a relatively free press, and the like). While, admittedly, none of these elements (or any combination of them) are *sufficient* to explain why political corruption proliferates in one country and not in another, it remains a fact that all of these elements were lacking in post-independence Ghana to a significant degree.

It can be argued that there may be other ways of dissipating public resources that are more unproductive and more economically devastating than acts of political corruption. Wars, crusades, spectacular diplomatic displays, state appropriations to maintain monarchies in luxury, arms races, and flights to the moon have all been denounced by critics as both fruitless and enormously expensive: Yet all these activities have their champions and where *raisons d'etat* are insufficient justification, economic necessity or the general public benefit are argued. Political corruption, on the other hand, has few defenders; even those who insist on its utility maintain not that it confers undiluted good, but that *some* corruption, or a little bit here and there, may have salutary consequences. While it is true that rich countries are usually better able to bear its effects, it also remains true that in the long run political corruption unchecked can ruin any polity; the fragile political and economic systems of the poorer, third world countries are simply much more vulnerable to its depradations.

Finally, we return to the problem of causes. In chapter 5 we argue that some of the explanations for political corruption in Ghana might lie in the transformation and perversion of traditional practices and attitudes, in certain aspects of the colonial heritage, in the rise of the "new men" to power, and in the unbalanced growth of post-independence institutions. Our argument is not that any or all of these factors necessarily caused Ghanaian political corruption, but that these factors must be taken into account in any attempt to explain the phenomenon. The same argument applies in principle, if not in detail, to other post-colonial polities, particularly those in Africa. James O'Connell takes us a step farther by arguing "a certain inevitability about the political instability in contemporary African countries [which] ... has to be lived through and coped with."[7] O'Connell suggests that in addition to the likelihood of post-independence power struggles (owing to "the artificiality of the colonial independence settlement"[8]) and the threat to government stability inherent in the economic problems facing new countries, the new ruling classes in several countries have proved unable to cope effectively with the demands and responsibilities of independence because a "talented generation was lost to politics."[9] That generation, which manned the institutional machinery during the transition period and therefore could not play an active role in politics, conceded the political battle (and thereby, the power) to the nationalist politicians.

> Thus [argues O'Connell], in the generation immediately behind the leading nationalists, many of the ablest talents were not available for political posts, and this weakened the ranks of the political class. The consequent loss only deepened the inadequacies of a generation of politicians who would in any case have found the transition from the struggle for power to the employment of power most difficult to make. The trouble was that many of these men were incompetent, corrupt, and communal.[10]

Ghana's "new men" certainly fit O'Connell's description of a generation of politicians unequal to their task, and many members of both the Ghanaian "colonial middle class" and the Ghanaian "colonial bureaucracy" could be counted as part of O'Connell's "lost" generation. In the event, the new ruling class proved unable to shift political gears from agitational, oppositional politics to effective rulership; in power its members behaved as if they were still on the outside clamoring to get in. They tended to treat opposition as subversion, and to see the institutional and constitutional restraints of the colonial settlement as calculated hindrances to their enjoyment of power. Almost inevitably, they came also to view political and governmental position as no more than their just due, and to consider political resources as theirs to dispose of as they saw fit. In O'Connell's words,

> They had little comprehension of how to assess resources, or how to make quantitative estimates of income and expenditure. They saw little reason why economic planning should not be "bent" to include projects which the economists said were unviable or over-expensive, but which they wanted to implement for reasons of prestige or personal profit.[11]

Again, the description applies to the "new men" of the Nkrumah era; and, by an ironic twist, it applies in some measure to the political class of the Busia regime as well. The latter group, an uneasy amalgam of "new men" exiled or fallen from grace during the Nkrumah regime and elements of the colonial middle class and colonial bureaucracy who had opposed Nkrumah from the start, behaved in much the same manner as the men they criticized before 1966. They were often arrogant, intolerant, and inept. In short, they manifested the same inability to abandon the attitudes that inure to men long out of power, the same inability to adjust from opposition to rulership.[12]

Finally, the corruption of the new class in Ghana and elsewhere may well be explained in good part by what O'Connell calls "the breakdown of trust and predictability in societies in transition."[13]

> In changing societies, this double breakdown brings in its train social hazards which are greater for politicians than for most other members of society. In an endeavor to buttress the predictability without which social living becomes hazardous, politicians sought to control the actions of individuals through the power of money.[14]

Money of course was only one of the kinds of resources available to reduce the uncertainties of transition and attain some measure of personal and political security. As we have seen, all the instruments of power—virtually all the political resources of the state and of office—came to be used for these purposes by the "new men" in Ghana, and at all echelons of the regime. The effects of this endeavor—on individuals, on the system, on rational decision-making—were devastating. The national morale eroded as more and more idealistic programs fell by the wayside and as private use of public resources became more and more flagrant. With that, the regime lost popular confidence to the point that it could not muster the support necessary for its survival in a time of crisis.

Appendix A

Reports of Commissions and Committees
of Inquiry Dealing with Corrupt Practices, 1957–71

(Bracketed designations are forms for short reference)

I. Nkrumah Period, 1956–66

1. *Report of the Commission of Enquiry into the Affairs of the Cocoa Purchasing Company, Ltd.* 1956. [Jibowu Commission]
2. *Report of the Commission Appointed to Enquire into the Circumstances Which Led to the Payment of £ 28,545 to James Colledge (Cocoa) Limited as Compensation for Land Acquired for the Achiasi-Kotoku Railway.* 1963. [Crabbe Commission]
3. *Report of the Commission of Enquiry into Alleged Irregularities and Malpractices in Connection with the Issue of Import Licenses.* 1964. [Akainyah Commission]
4. *Report of the Commission of Inquiry into Mr. Braimah's Resignation and Allegations Arising Therefrom.* 1954. [Korsah Commission]
5. *Report of the Commission of Enquiry into Trade Malpractices in Ghana.* 1965. [Abraham Commission]

II. NLC and Second Republic Period, 1966–1972; NRC Period 1972–?

1. *Report of the Committee of Inquiry on the Local Purchasing of Cocoa.* 1966. [De Graft-Johnson Committee]
2. *Report of the Commission of Inquiry on the Commercial Activities of the Erstwhile Publicity Secretariat.* 1966. [Ayeh Commission]. White Paper: W.P. No. 3/66.

115

3. *Report of the Commission to Enquire into the Affairs of NADECO Limited.* 1966. [Azu Crabbe Commission]. White Paper: W.P. No. 1/66.

4. *Report of the Commission to Enquire into the Kwame Nkrumah Properties.* 1967. [Apaloo Commission]

5. *Report of the Commission of Enquiry into Irregularities and Malpractices in the Grant of Import Licenses.* 1967. And *Summary of the Report . . . Import Licenses.* 1967. [Ollenu Commission]. White Paper: W.P. No. 4/67.

6. *Report on the Audit Investigations into the Accounts of the Central Organization of Sport.* 1967. [Central Organization of Sport Investigation]

7. *The Tibo Committee Report on Ghana Sports.* 1967. [Tibo Committee]

8. *Report of the Commission of Enquiry into the Circumstances Surrounding the Establishment of the Ghana Cargo Handling Company.* 1967. [Korantang-Addow Commission]

9. *Report of the Commission of Enquiry into the Affairs of the Ghana Timber Marketing Board and the Ghana Timber Cooperative Union.* 1967. [Timber Commission]. White Paper: W.P. No. 11/68.

10. *Report of the Committee of Enquiry into the State Furniture and Joinery Corporation.* 1967. [Tsegah Committee]

11. *Report of the Commission of Inquiry, University of Science and Technology, Kumasi.* 1967. (J. S. Manyo-Plange, Chmn.) [UST Commission]

12. *Report of the Commission of Enquiry into Electoral and Local Government Reform.* Vol. I, Parts I and II, 1967; Vol. 2, Part III, 1968. [Siriboe Commission]

13. *Report of the Committee of Enquiry into the Affairs First Ghana Building Society.* 1968. [Boison Committee]

14. *Report of the Commission of Enquiry into the Funds of the Ghana Trades Union Congress.* 1968. [Munifie Commission]

15. *Report of the Committee Appointed to Enquire into the Manner of Operation of the State Distilleries Corporation.* 1968. [Taylor Committee]

16. *Report of the Commission Appointed to Enquire into the Manner of Operation of the State Housing Corporation.* 1968. [Effah Commission]

17. [*Report of the*] *Commission of Inquiry into Conditions in*

Ghana Prisons. 1968. [Prisons Commission]

18. *Report of the Commission Appointed to Enquire into the Functions, Operation, and Administration of the Workers Brigade.* 1968. [Kom Commission]

19. *Report of the Sowah Commission—Assets of Specified Persons.* Vol. I, 1968. Vols. II and III, 1971. [Sowah Commission]. White Paper: W.P. No. 16/69.

20. *Report of the Manyo—Plange Commission—Assets of Specified Persons.* 1968. [Manyo-Plange Commission]. White Paper: W.P. No. 11/69.

21. *Report of the Jiagge Commission—Assets of Specified Persons.* Vols. I–III, 1968–69. [Jiagge Commission]. White Paper: W.P. No. 3/69.

22. *Report of the Investigating Team Which Probed into the Star Publishing Company and the Guinea Press, Limited.* 1969. [Quist Team]

23. *Report of the Committee of Enquiry into the Affairs of the State Publishing Corporation.* 1969. [Essah Committee]

24. *Report of the Commission of Enquiry into the Affairs of the Kumasi City Council.* 1969. [Totoe Commission]

25. *Report of the Committee Appointed to Enquire into the Allocation of the Keta Market Stalls and Other Ancillary Matters.* 1969. [Keta Committee]

26. *Interim and Final Reports of the Commission of Enquiry into the Accra-Tema City Council.* 1969. [Accra-Tema Commission]

27. *Report of the Commission Appointed under Act 250 to Enquire into the Affairs of the Sekondi-Takoradi City Council.* 1970. [Gaisie Commission]

28. *Report of the Committee of Enquiry on the Erstwhile Football Pools Authority.* 1971. [Osei-Hwere Committee]

29. *First, Second, and Third Interim Reports of the Commission of Inquiry into Bribery and Corruption.* 1972. [Anin Commission]. (This Committee was constituted in 1970, held hearings during 1970 and 1971, had its work interrupted by the January 1972 coup, then continued its work into 1972 and 1973. A final report was expected in 1973.)

III. Commissions of Inquiry that had not publicly reported by December 31, 1973.

1. [Special] Committee to Inquire into the Assets of Specified Persons. [Taylor Assets Committee] (Appointed in February 1972 by the NRC to investigate the assets of Dr. Busia and various ministers and functionaries. It still had not yet reported by the end of 1973.)

2. Commission of Inquiry, University of Ghana, Legon. (Constituted in 1968, this Commission issued its report in 1970. That report has not been made public, although copies are available for the perusal of teaching and administrative members of the University. It contains, among other matters, details of the corrupt dealings of a former Finance Officer of the University.)

3. Commission of Enquiry into the State Fisheries Corporation. (Constituted, according to reports, in 1966, this Commission submitted its report in 1969. The report was never made public because, according to a former director of the Corporation, it contained too much material incriminating key officials of the Busia government.)

4. [Parliamentary] Commission to Inquire into the Sale of Soviet-built Trawlers. (This Commission was constituted in 1970 to inquire into the sale of ten trawlers originally purchased by the government from the Soviet Union and then sold to an English businessman for $120,000, which it is claimed was one-tenth of their original value. The transaction took place during the NLC period, and was challenged in May 1970 when the purchaser, a Mr. Victor Passer, was about to claim the ships.)

5. Committee of Enquiry into the Lease of Certain Lands to Ejura Farms, Limited. (This Committee was constituted in 1970; its primary question was whether a lease executed by the Ejurahene—traditional chief of the area—was irregular, particularly since large sums of money allegedly were paid the Ejurahene during the transaction.)

6. Committee to Investigate the Affairs of the Asamankese Local Council. (Constituted in 1970; this Committee apparently reported in May 1971, but its report was not made public. Its chairman

was C. E. Fiscian, head of the Department of Psychology, University of Ghana.)
7. Commission of Inquiry into the Affairs of the Kumasi City Council.
   (Constituted in February 1971, this Commission followed upon the heels of dismissal of the 16-man Management Committee of the Kumasi City Council and the appointment of the Interim Management Committee. The Commission held regular hearings until May 1971, when "the enthusiasm in the whole proceedings waned when its chairman, Mr. Cann, suffered electric shock while he held the microphone to question a witness." *Ghanaian Times*, June 16, 1971, p. 4)
8. (Intra-Ministry) Committee to Investigate Allegations of Bribery, Corruption, Maladministration, and Nepotism in the Ministry of Education.
   (Constituted in December 1970 at the order of Minister of Education William Ofori-Ata; the Committee held all of its meetings *in camera* during 1971. Its findings were not reported publicly, although, presumably, it tendered its report to the minister.)
9. Commission of Inquiry into the Administration of University College, Cape Coast.
   (This Commission was appointed in 1966 and submitted its report sometime during 1970.)
10–22. Special audit investigations ordered in 1966 by the National Liberation Council into the finances of:
10. The Convention Peoples' Party
11. The Ghana Young Pioneer Movement
12. The United Ghana Farmers' Cooperative Council
13. The Central Organization of Sports
14. The Ghana Muslim Council
15. The Ideological Institute, Winneba
16. The Workers' Brigade
17. The African Affairs Centre
18. The Bureau of African Affairs
19. The State Cocoa Marketing Board
20. The National Council of Ghana Women
21. The Young Farmers' League
22. The Tobacco Products Corporation

Reports of these investigations were filed in 1967. No. 13 was published as the Report on the Central Organization of Sports–see item II, 6 above–and nos. 15, 17, and 18 apparently were used in preparing two pamphlets issued in 1968: *Nkrumah's Deception of Africa* and *Nkrumah's Subversion in Africa*. No. 12 apparently was incorporated into the De Graft-Johnson Committee report–see II, 1 above.

23. Investigating Committee into the Assets of Certain CPP Functionaries, Ministers, and Members of Parliament.

    (On May 8, 1961, one month following President Nkrumah's "Dawn Broadcast," he appointed a committee headed by Sir Charles Tachie-Benson to investigate the assets of various ministers and officials. The committee, according to Geoffrey Bing, former attorney-general of Ghana, reported on June 16, 1961, but its report, though printed and ready for distribution, was never published because of the strong opposition of one minister, Tawiah Adamafio. Instead, Nkrumah issued a statement announcing that he had asked for the resignation of six ministers, and demanded that six others divest themselves of properties in excess of a combined value of £ G20,000. For particulars, see Geoffrey Bing, *Reap the Whirlwind*, London: MacGibbon and Kee, 1968, pp. 407–8; and Government of Ghana, *Statement by the President Concerning Properties and Business Connections of Ministers and Ministerial Secretaries*, W. P. no. 6/61, September 29, 1961.)

24. Commission of Inquiry into the Affairs of the Black Star Line.

    (Appointed in 1966.)

25. Commission of Inquiry into the Affairs of the State Diamond Mining Corporation. (Appointed in 1967(?); its report was submitted, but as of December 31, 1973, not yet published. See Republic of Ghana, *Parliamentary Debates, Official Report*, Vol. 3, No. 5 [Tuesday, May 19, 1970], Accra: Ghana Publishing Corp, 1970. Cols. 95–97.

Appendix B

1. Excerpts from Civil Service Act. 1960. C.A. 5

Part V. Misconduct and Unsatisfactory Service

(Sec.) 25. (1) Any act done without reasonable excuse by a Civil Servant which amounts fo a failure to perform in a proper manner any duty imposed upon him as such, or which contravenes any enactment relating to the Civil Service, or which is otherwise prejudicial to the efficient conduct of the Civil Service or tends to bring the Civil Service into disrepute shall constitute misconduct;. . .

26. It is misconduct for a Civil Servant . . .

    (c) to use, without the consent of the prescribed authority, any property or facilities provided for the purposes of the Civil Service for some purpose not connected with his official duties; . . .

    (e) to engage in any gainful occupation outside the Civil Service without the consent of the prescribed authority.

2. Excerpts from Civil Service Disciplinary Code Regulations, 1971. C.I. 17

Part I. Discipline and Penalties

(Sec) 1. (1) Any act done without reasonable excuse by a Civil Servant, which amounts to failure to perform in a proper manner any duty imposed upon him as such or which contravenes any of the provisions of any Regulations or enactment relating to the Civil Service, or which is otherwise prejudicial to the efficient conduct of the Civil Service or tends to bring the Civil Service into disrepute shall constitute, and shall render the offending Civil Servant liable to disciplinary action.

121

Part III. Explanatory Note on Certain Types of Misconduct

20. (1) No Civil Servant shall receive presents in any form in the course of his duties which may have the effect of influencing his decision, nor may he receive any compensation or reward for the performance of any official duties except as approved by government.

(2) A Civil Servant shall not give presents to other Civil Servants which may influence them in matters in which he is interested.

(3) This paragraph applies not only to the Civil Servant and his friends, but also to his dependents and family, and he shall be responsible for its observance by his dependents and family.

21. No Civil Servant shall in his personal capacity receive any payment from public funds on behalf of or as an agent for any member of the public.

23. (1) No Civil Servant shall engage in paid employment outside his official duties or when on leave except with the express permission of the Secretary to the Cabinet through his Head of Department or Class.

24. (1) No Civil servant shall engage in any business except with the express permission of the Secretary of the Cabinet.

(4) A Civil Servant shall on appointment declare any interest he may have in any business undertaking.

Schedule—Acts of Misconduct

1. Fraud.
2. Falsification of records.
3. Leakage of information prejudicial to the interest of the State.
6. Stealing.
7. Dishonesty.
8. Taking confidential information to private person.
12. Giving and receiving of presents and gifts.
13. Obtaining material on fraudulent orders or misrepresentation.
15. Acting as private agent.
17. Wilful damage to government property.
18. Engaging in any activity outside his official duties which are likely to . . . lead to his taking improper advantage of his position in the Civil Service.

19. Engaging in gainful occupation outside the service without consent.
20. Engaging in business without consent.
23. Use of machinery, vehicle or equipment without authority.
24. Careless dissipation of government property.
35. Failure to obtain permission to attend unofficial activities during office hours.
36. Money lending.

Notes

Introduction

1. The author spent the academic years 1969–70, 1970–71 at the University of Ghana as Head of the Department of Political Science.

2. B. K. Adama, Ghanaian Minister of State for Parliamentary Affairs, referred at one time to "the reports of 76 Commissions of Enquiry" that "have so far been published." (Ghana) *Parliamentary Debates*, Wednesday, 24 June 1970, col. 1164. Whether Adama was thinking of all the Commissions of Inquiry reports published since 1945, or just those published since the 1966 coup, is not clear. As nearly complete a list as I was able to compile is found in Appendix A of this study.

3. Nkrumah himself was not prone to apologize for his own or other people's behavior. The closest he came to an attempt at self-justification is the book he wrote just after the 1966 coup: *Dark Days in Ghana* (New York: International Publishers, 1968). Other works about his regime include Geoffrey Bing, *Reap the Whirlwind* (London: MacGibbon and Kee, 1968); Samuel Ikoku, *Le Ghana de Kwame Nkrumah* (Paris: François Maspéro, 1971); Bob Fitch and Mary Oppenheimer, "Ghana: End of an Illusion," *Monthly Review* 18, no. 3 (July-August 1966); David Apter, *Ghana in Transition*, 2d ed. (New Haven: Yale University Press, 1972); W. Scott Thompson, *Ghana's Foreign Policy, 1957–1966* (Princeton, N.J.: Princeton University Press, 1969); Roger Genoud, *Nationalism and Economic Development in Ghana* (New York: Frederick Praeger, 1969); Henry L. Bretton, *The Rise and Fall of Kwame Nkrumah* (New York: Frederick Praeger, 1966); and T. Peter Omari, *Kwame Nkrumah: The Anatomy of an African Dictatorship* (Accra: Moxon Paperbacks, 1970).

4. Nathaniel H. Leff, "Economic Development Through Bureaucratic Corruption," *American Behavioral Scientist* 8, no. 3

(November 1964): 8–14; Joseph S. Nye, "Corruption and Political Development: A Cost-Benefit Analysis," *American Political Science Review* 61, no. 2 (June 1967):417–27.

5. See James C. Scott, *Comparative Political Corruption* (Englewood Cliffs, N.J.: Prentice-Hall, 1972).

1: Political Corruption:
An Outline of a Model

1. What is here termed "political" corruption has been styled "bureaucratic" or "official" corruption by others who view officials and bureaucrats as necessary factors in the process. The choice is perhaps a matter of taste, but "political" is used here to avoid the possible inference that corruption *begins* with officials or bureaucrats. Officials may, of course, initiate corrupt transactions, or they may be drawn in by persons already involved in corrupt activities outside the formal polity. Or simply, the offer to engage in a politically corrupt transaction may be made by someone other than an official.

What I have called "apolitical" corruption should not be confused with Scott's "market" and "parochial" types of corruption. "As ideal types," states Scott, "'parochial' (non-market) corruption is a situation where only ties of kinship, affection, caste, and so forth determine access to the favors of power-holders, whereas 'market' corruption signifies an impersonal process in which influence is accorded those who can 'pay' the most, regardless of who they are." James C. Scott, *Comparative Political Corruption* (Englewood Cliffs, N.J.: Prentice-Hall, 1972), p. 88. Obviously, both "market" and "parochial" corruption can affect both the informal and the formal systems in the polity, as they can also affect both the formal polity and the private sectors of society.

2. My discussion of political goods and resources derives in part from Warren F. Ilchman and Norman Thomas Uphoff, *The Political Economy of Change* (Berkeley: University of California Press, 1969), particularly chapter 3.

3. Gabriel A. Almond and G. Bingham Powell, Jr., *Comparative Politics: A Developmental Approach* (Boston: Little, Brown, 1966), pp. 198–99.

4. Although this distinction is admittedly somewhat arbitrary, it does have at least one important consequence: it permits us to disengage from the core of our discussion that most common conversion of public goods, the so-called white collar crime. White collar crimes include the innumerable ordinary individual acts of thievery and misappropriation that plague governmental institutions great and small everywhere. We recognize that such acts, if repeated or habitual, may lead to political corruption; we also recognize that white-collar crime may in fact have considerable impact on a political system, particularly if the cost of the political resources taken or misused is so high as to frustrate the attainment of socially desirable ends. For purposes of this study, however, such crime is viewed as a datum in the analysis of the causes and consequences of political corruption, but its presence is deemed neither necessary nor sufficient to establish political corruption.

5. Specific examples that illustrate transactions of some structural complexity are provided in chapter 4.

6. See Gabriel A. Almond and Sidney Verba, *The Civic Culture* (Princeton, N.J.: Princeton University Press, 1963) *passim*; and Richard E. Dawson and Kenneth Prewitt, *Political Socialization* (Boston: Little, Brown, 1969), pp. 25–36.

7. See Victor T. LeVine, "The Political Cultures of French-Speaking Africa," *Ghana Social Science Journal* 1, no. 2 (November 1971):63–79.

8. See, for example, Merle Kling, "Violence and Politics in Latin America," *The Sociological Review Monograph*, no. 11: "Latin-American Sociological Studies," University of Keele (England), February 1967, pp. 119–32.

9. It should be noted that our stress is on *politically corrupt* networks of relationships, not on the complex of social networks that exist in any society, whatever its political culture. A culture of political corruption may, of course, develop with existing social networks as its base, the participants acquiring and spreading the values consonant with the growth and maintenance of politically corrupt relationships. Or individuals with these values may build their own networks of relationships, which in turn may intersect or parallel networks operating on different premises. In any case, while we recognize the universality of non-corrupt social networks, it is only those special

relationships involving the self-serving disposition of public resources that concern us here.

10. See, for example, F. G. Bailey, "Parapolitical Systems," in Marc J. Swartz, ed., *Local-Level Politics* (Chicago: Aldine, 1968), pp. 281-94. The question of how and whether parapolitical systems relate to informal polities is further explored in chapter 4, as are ancillary questions concerning the extent of the informal polity.

11. The possibility of a Ghanaian informal polity is considered in chapter 4.

12. The case of Indonesia serves as a good example. Here, in addition to the Indonesian national political system—which might be termed the "archipelagian" system—there is a separate political system for each of the insular components (Java, Sumatra, etc.). It probably would not be difficult to demonstrate the existence of an Indonesian "archipelagian" informal polity operating almost synchronically (or in this case perhaps synonymously) with the national polity. Given the pervasiveness of political corruption in the Indonesian political culture and the probability of an "archipelagian" informal polity, the existence of informal subpolities in the insular subsystems can almost be assumed.

13. John Waterbury, "Endemic and Planned Corruption in a Monarchical Regime," *World Politics* 25, no. 4 (July 1973):534.

14. *Ibid.*, p. 547.

2: The Culture of Political Corruption

1. Aiken Watson, Chairman, *Report of the Commission to Inquire into Disturbances in the Gold Coast* (London: HMSO, 1948), p. 8 Hereafter cited as Watson Commission Report.

2. "Corruption in African Public Life," *Legon Observer* 1, no. 5 (2 September 1966):7. *The Legon Observer* is published by a group of academicians at the University of Ghana, Legon.

3. M. J. Sharpston, "The Economics of Corruption," *New Society* (London), 26 November 1970, p. 944.

4. From an interview in April 1971. Mr. J. was one of a dozen highly placed former officials interviewed by the author during 1970-71. Since these persons were admittedly involved in the large-

scale corruption of the Nkrumah regime, they must remain anonymous.

5. James C. Scott, *Comparative Political Corruption* (Englewood Cliffs, N.J.: Prentice-Hall, 1972), p. 81. See also W. F. Wertheim, "Sociological Aspects of Corruption in Southeast Asia," *Sociologica Neerlandica* 1, no. 2 (Autumn 1963):129–52, reprinted in Arnold J. Heidenheimer, *Political Corruption* (New York: Holt, Rinehart and Winston, 1970), pp. 195–211.

6. Scott, *Comparative Political Corruption*, p. 82.

7. *Ibid.*

8. *Ibid.*

9. *Ibid.*, pp. 84–86. My use of the term "self-perpetuating" is not accidental. The oligarchy neatly solved the problem of transition posed by the death of dictator François Duvalier in 1971 by decreeing that his under-age son, Jean-Claude, was in fact twenty-one, and then making him the new president for life. Thus, the system that Duvalier brought to corrupt perfection continues unchanged.

10. See David Wurfel, "The Philippines," in Richard Rose and Arnold J. Heidenheimer, eds., "Comparative Studies in Political Finance: A Symposium," *Journal of Politics* 25, no. 4 (November 1963): 757–73; Albert Ravenholt, "The Peso Price of Politics," *AUFS Reports, Southeast Asia Series*, no. 6 (May 1958):40.

11. Stanislas Andreski, *The African Predicament* (New York: Atherton, 1968), pp. 92–109. For a vivid account of the Western Nigerian situation, see Richard Sklar, "The Ordeal of Chief Awolowo," in G. M. Carter, ed., *Politics in Africa—7 cases* (New York: Harcourt, Brace and World, 1966), pp. 119–66.

12. An unidentified lecturer quoted by David Finlay in "The Ghana Coup," an unpublished paper (1966), p. 9.

13. Beverly J. Pooley, "Corruption and Development in Ghana," unpublished paper (1969); quotation by permission of the author.

14. Scott, *Comparative Political Corruption*, p. 30.

15. T. Peter Omari, *Kwame Nkrumah: The Anatomy of an African Dictatorship* (Accra: Moxon Paperbacks, 1970).

16. Henry Bretton, *The Rise and Fall of Kwame Nkrumah: A Study of Personal Rule in Africa* (New York: Frederick Praeger, 1966).

17. Until the 1955–56 *Report*, the territory's fiscal year ran from

April 1 until March 31; in 1956, the fiscal year was changed to run from July 1 to June 30, and in 1962 it was changed again to run from October 1 to September 30. The audit reports for 1949–50, 1953–54, 1956–57, 1958–59, 1959–60, and 1963–64 were not available for consultation. The general reports will hereafter be cited by the shortened form, "*Report, 19   –   *", unless a special audit report is noted. Full citations are as follows:

Gold Coast Colony, *Report of the Auditor for the Year 1938–39* (Accra, 1940); reports for succeeding years have the same title; dates of publication are in parentheses: 1939–40(1940), 1940–41 (1942), 1942–43(1944), 1943–44(1945), 1944–45(1946), 1945–46 (1946), 1946–47(1948).

Gold Coast Colony, *Report of the Director of Audit for the Financial Year Ended 31st March, 1948* (Accra, 1949); succeeding reports have the same title; dates of publication are in parentheses: 1948–49(1950), 1949–50(1951).

Gold Coast, *Report of the Director of Audit on the Accounts of the Gold Coast for the Financial Year Ending 31st March, 1951* (Accra, 1952); reports for succeeding years have the same title; dates of publication are in parentheses: 1951–52(1953), 1952–53(1954), 1953–54 (1955), 1954–55(1956).

Gold Coast, *Report of the Auditor-General on the Accounts of the Gold Coast for the Financial Period Ended 30th June, 1956* (Accra, 1957); covers 15 mos. The 1956–57 report had the same title, was published in 1958.

Ghana, *Report of the Auditor-General on the Accounts of Ghana for the Financial Year Ended 30th June, 1958* (Accra, 1960); reports through 1961 had the same title; dates of publication are in parentheses: 1958–59(1960), 1959–60(1961), 1960–61(1962).

Ghana, *Report and Financial Statements by the Accountant-General and Report Thereon by the Auditor-General for the Year Ended 30th September, 1962* (Accra, 1965); the 1962–63 report had the same title, and was published in 1965.

Ghana, *Report by the Auditor-General on the Accounts of Ghana for the Period 1st January, 1965 to 30th June, 1966* (Accra, 1968); covers 18 months.

Ghana, *Report by the Auditor-General on the Accounts of Ghana: First Report for 1971, Local Authorities and Educational Institutions,*

1967–68, 1968–69 (Accra, 1971). *Second Report for 1971, Treasury Accounts, 1967–68, 1968–69* (Accra, 1971). *Third Report for 1971, Public Boards and Corporations, 1967–68, 1968–69* (Accra, 1971). Our analysis of the reports begins with 1938 simply because the pre-1938 reports were unavailable, either in Ghana or abroad.

18. It was claimed that the chairman of the Kumasi City Council bribed field auditors of the auditor-general's staff to overlook the persistent shortages in council accounts during the Nkrumah period. Totoe Commission, pp. 68–72.

19. *Report, 1950–51*, p. 9.

20. Watson Commission Report, p. 42, para. 218. This aspect of the Watson Report, and the later revelations of the Abraham Commission (1965) are discussed on pp. 25–26.

21. *Report, 1954–55*, p. 17.

22. The associations involving cocoa production and marketing were particularly important. For a comment, see Dennis Austin, *Politics in Ghana, 1946–60* (London: Oxford University Press, 1964), p. 65.

23. Market cartels in West Africa are surveyed by Marvin Miracle, "Market Structure and Conduct in Tropical Africa: A Survey," in Sayre P. Schatz, ed., *South of the Sahara: Development in African Economies* (Philadelphia: Temple University Press, 1972), pp. 92–101. The structure and activities of the marketing boards are covered in detail in Peter T. Bauer, *West African Trade* (London: Routledge and Kegan Paul, 1963), pp. 263–378.

24. Austin, *Politics in Ghana*, pp. 172–73. For details of the CPC–CPP links, see the Jibowu Commission report.

25. John Waterbury, "Endemic and Planned Corruption in a Monarchical Regime," *World Politics* 25, no. 4 (July 1973):538.

26. *Report, 1955–56*, p. 8.

27. *Report, 1957–58*, p. 17.

28. The list and quotations are from pp. 19–22 of the *Report, 1960–61*.

29. *Report, 1962–63*, p. 17. See also *First and Second Report from the Public Accounts Committee of the National Assembly, . . . with Debates Thereon* (Accra, 1965), pp. 53–54.

30. *Report, 1965–66,* pp. 18–19, ss. 113–16.

31. *First and Second Report from the Public Accounts Committee . . . ,* p. 80.

32. *Ibid.,* pp. 81–82. Kusi had to retract his second reference to Nkrumah, but stood by the rest. His statement has additional bite when the reference to "international schools" is clarified: these are *private* schools in Ghana, some of long standing, which cater to the children of diplomats, foreign residents, and wealthy Ghanaians. Tuition tends to be high and entrance requirements stiff; the combined effect is that they are schools expressly catering to the social, political, and economic elite. Their "international" character also contributes to their snob appeal. It should be added that Kusi was a former member of the opposition United Party.

33. Bretton, *The Rise and Fall of Kwame Nkrumah,* p. 69. I do not agree with Bretton that the committee dealt mostly with petty theft and the mismanagement of modest public funds. Its investigation of corrupt dealings in the Ghana Educational Trust (involving funds up to £ G2 million), and its commentary on massive squandering of funds in the Foreign Ministry (involving hundreds of thousands of Ghanaian pounds) hardly suggests a preoccupation with small matters. It did, to be sure, withhold comment on the more notable, and visible, corruption at the highest echelons.

34. Documentation of these cases is as follows (a shortened form for later citation is included in each item):

Sir Arku Korsah, Commissioner, *Report of the Commission of Inquiry into Mr. Braimah's Resignation and Allegations Arising Therefrom* (Accra, 1954). [Korsah Commission]

O. Jibowu, Chairman, *Report of the Commission of Enquiry into the Affairs of the Cocoa Purchasing Company, Ltd.* (Accra, 1956). [Jibowu Commission]

A. A. Akainyah, Commissioner, *Report of the Commission of Enquiry into Alleged Irregularities and Malpractices in Connection with the Issue of Import Licenses* (Accra, 1964). [Akainyah Commission]

W. E. Abraham, Chairman, *Report of the Commission of Enquiry into Trade Malpractices in Ghana* (Accra, 1965). [Abraham Commission]

Statement by the President Concerning Properties and Business

Connections of Ministers and Ministerial Secretaries (Accra, September 1961). For additional references see Appendix A, III, 23.

35. Jibowu Commission; Bretton, *The Rise and Fall of Kwame Nkrumah*, p. 69; Omari, *Kwame Nkrumah* pp. 41–42.

36. *Report of the Commission of Enquiry into Irregularities and Malpractices in the Grant of Import Licenses* (Accra, 1967); and *Summary of the Report.* . . . [Ollenu Commission]

37. Akainyah Commission, p. 38

38. Ollenu Commission, *Summary*, p. 12. Akainyah interceded with Nkrumah, the attorney-general, Kwaw Swanzy, and the minister of trade, Kwesi Armah, on behalf of one Obed Mensah who had appeared before the Akainyah Commission and admitted forging an import license. Mensah claimed that because of his testimony before the Akainyah Commission his firm had been blacklisted, and that consequently he could not get another import license. Apparently, Akainyah, A. Y. K. Djin, and Armah advised Mensah to change the name of his firm, which he did; he was thereupon given a license by Armah. It also transpired that Mensah was Akainyah's "ward." Justice Ollenu, in the face of these confusing facts, was lenient toward Akainyah, arguing that although Akainyah "was aware of the fraud" (of Mensah's changing the firm name), he (Akainyah) was falsely convinced that an injustice was being done to his ward and felt constrained to help him. Mensah also acted as sub-agent for Justice Akainyah's wife in demanding and collecting bribes from several business firms in connection with the issue of import licenses. Mrs. Akainyah's house was described as "a clearing house for illegal transactions: bribery and corruption in connection with import licenses"; and Akainyah himself was accused of taking bribes (p. 22).

39. Ollenu Commission, para. 146. The Akainyah report bears evidence of the excision: though the paragraphs are numbered consecutively throughout the report, the chapters are numbered One, Two, and Four; moreover paragraph 12 mentions a Chapter Three, but no Chapter Three exists in the published version.

40. Bretton, *The Rise and Fall of Kwame Nkrumah*, p. 214, no. 42, citing Kweku Akwei's article in the *Evening News*, March 25, 1966.

41. Abraham Commission, pp. 78–79. The pass-book system was instituted in the 1940s as a device by which various wholesale and retail companies could keep records of their dealings with petty

traders; it was intended as a check on profiteering and hoarding when supplies were in short supply. Abuses of this practice in 1948 came in for comment in the Watson Commission Report, which recommended that a system of state-controlled retail outlets be created to curb these problems. GNTC (with over 150 outlets in 1964) was to have been that solution; as it turned out, GNTC officials simply took over the pass-book system and ran it for their own benefit. The GNCC was the state construction corporation, which operated sales offices in various parts of the country.

42. Geoffrey Bing, *Reap the Whirlwind* (London: MacGibbon and Kee, 1968), pp. 406-8.

43. Omari, *Kwame Nkrumah*, p. 66.

44. Geoffrey Bing understood the contradictory nature of this phenomenon: ". . . men like Krobo Edusei were still intensely popular. If they were corrupt, it was the foreigner from whom they extorted money and Krobo Edusei's generosity to Ghanaians in need was proverbial." *Reap the Whirlwind*, p. 409. What Bing either failed to see or refused to acknowledge was the cumulative effect of corrupt behavior on public opinion—satiation, then angry frustration—and the fact that Edusei and his colleagues extorted not only from foreigners but from Ghanaians as well.

45. One internationally bruited incident, for example, involved the purchase of a gold-plated bed by the wife of Agriculture Minister Krobo Edusei. This story received a great deal of attention in Ghana and bears retelling. Early in 1962, Mrs. Edusei saw a magnificent bed in a London furniture store: it consisted of a king-size frame with gold-plated head and footboards, and canopy, pillows, and bed-cover of gold cloth. The price was $8,400. She ordered the bed shipped to the Edusei home in Accra. News of the purchase reached Nkrumah, who thereupon reminded his minister of the message of the Dawn Broadcast. Edusei reportedly ordered his wife to return the bed to the seller, pointing out that a gold-plated $8,400 bed hardly suited the life style of the wife of a dedicated socialist. At first Mrs. Edusei refused, but when Accra newspapers began commenting on it she capitulated. One of the more entertaining accounts of the "Golden Bed" affair is in "Les Mauvais draps," *Afrique Nouvelle*, 15–21 April 1962.

46. This point emerged in a series of talk sessions between the author and a number of Ghanaian officers at Teshie Camp during 1970 and 1971.

47. This is Joseph S. Nye's judgment; see his "Corruption and Political Development: A Cost-Benefit Analysis," *American Political Science Review* 61, no. 2 (June 1967):417, wherein he dismisses the Commissions of Inquiry as "post-coup rationalizations." Herbert H. Werlin cites Jon Kraus, "Arms and Politics in Ghana," in Claude E. Welch, ed., *Soldier and State in Africa* (Evanston: Northwestern University Press, 1970), pp. 188–89, to reinforce his own observations of the commissions' "judiciousness and fairness." See Werlin, "The Roots of Corruption—The Ghanaian Enquiry," *Journal of Modern African Studies* 10, no. 2 (1972):252, n. 4.

48. See Bing, *Reap the Whirlwind*; and Samuel G. Ikoku (pseud. Julius Sago), *Le Ghana de Kwame Nkrumah* (Paris: François Maspéro, 1971), pp. 107–11: "Nkrumah n'etait pas corrumpu."

49. W. Scott Thompson, *Ghana's Foreign Policy, 1957–1966* (Princeton, N.J.: Princeton University Press, 1969), p. 269. Thompson is quoting an unidentified interviewee; he (Thompson) identifies Immanuel Ayeh Kumi as "the very rich Nzima advisor of Nkrumah's who was widely considered notoriously corrupt" (p. 269, fn. 14). Ayeh Kumi figured prominently in several of the Commissions of Inquiry: he was Nkrumah's economic adviser, and also, as chairman of NADECO, was responsible for funneling extorted moneys to Nkrumah and the CPP.

50. See F. K. Apaloo, Chairman, *Report of the Commission to Enquire into the Kwame Nkrumah Properties* (Accra, 1967); hereafter cited as Apaloo Commission. The Apaloo Commission found that at the time of the coup Nkrumah was worth £ 2,322,009 Os 10d in cash and physical assets. Ikoku, *Le Ghana de Nkrumah*, disagrees, claiming that the commission included in its estimates property belonging not only to Nkrumah but to the state as well, and that it wrongly attributed certain overseas properties to him (including houses in Cairo and Tunis). Ikoku contends that in fact Nkrumah in 1966 owned goods, property, and cash worth no more than £ 363,000. Ikoku, of course, has his own reasons for wishing to clear Nkrumah of wrong-doing: he was himself closely involved with the regime, and he has advanced the thesis that imperialist machinations, not flaws in the system, were responsible for Nkrumah's downfall. Ikoku also points out in the ex-President's defense that the CPP was the beneficiary in Nkrumah's will. The will to which Ikoku refers is Nkrumah's second will; the first was much more conventional, disposing his property to

various relatives and friends. There is some question whether the second was not merely "window dressing," as a Ghanaian lawyer suggested to me in 1969. For texts of both wills, see Omari, *Kwame Nkrumah*, pp. 215–20.

51. Apaloo Commission, pp. 30–39. Appendix 10 of the Apaloo Report, pp. 142–43, indicates that another £ 10,000 from the same transaction was deposited "for Fathia" (Nkrumah's Egyptian wife), and that still another £ 80,000 "was brought and given to Ex-President Nkrumah by Wm. Q. Halm in American dollars on return from Switzerland" (Leventis had deposited £ 170,000 of the principal in the Swiss Credit Bank in the names of Halm and Ayeh Kumi, Nkrumah's agents.)

52. *Ibid.*, p. 24. The glider was given to the glider school run by Hanna Reitsch, a German aviatrix at one time much honored by the Nazi hierarchy for her exploits. Nkrumah brought her to Ghana to establish the school. She later published an account of her Ghanaian experiences: *Ich flog fur Kwame Nkrumah* [I flew for Kwame Nkrumah] (Munich: Lehman, 1968).

53. Bing, *Reap the Whirlwind*, pp. 408–10. Bing blames pressures from the "industrial side of the Party" and the Civil Service for Nkrumah's unwillingness to institute a wholesale housecleaning.

54. Ikoku, *Le Ghana de Nkrumah*, p. 111. Translation is mine.

55. For NADECO investigation, see S. Azu Crabbe, Chairman, *Report of the Commission to Enquire into the Affairs of NADECO Limited* (Accra, 1966) [Azu Crabbe Commission]. NADECO was considered by the Apaloo Commission to have been a "de facto" property of Nkrumah; a special audit on NADECO is reported on pp. 89–105 of the Apaloo Commission report.

For Guinea Press, see Cromwell C. Quist, Chairman, *Report of the Investigating Team Which Probed Into the Star Publishing Company and the Guinea Press, Ltd.* (Accra, 1969) [Quist Team]. The Press finances are detailed on pp. 114–27 of the Apaloo Commission report.

For NAPADO, see F. R. Ayeh, Chairman, *Report of the Commission of Inquiry on the Commercial Activities of the Erstwhile Publicity Secretary* (Accra, 1966), [Ayeh Commission], pp. 5–21.

For Ghana Bottling Company, Ltd., see Apaloo Commission report, which also named this company as one of Nkrumah's "de facto" properties; findings of a special audit of its accounts are on pp. 129–33.

56. Quist Team, p. 29.

57. *Ibid.*, p. 7.

58. *White Paper on the Report of the Commission of Inquiry into the Affairs of NADECO Limited,* no. 1/66 (Accra, 1966), pp. 3–4, 31–33.

59. Azu Crabbe Commission, p. 7, para. 32. The information given in the rest of this paragraph is from the same report.

60. *White Paper on the Report of the Commission of Enquiry into Alleged Irregularities and Malpractices in Connection with the Grant of Import Licenses,* no. 4/67 (Accra, 1967), p. 6.

61. These sums were obtained by adding the figures provided in the Azu Crabbe Commission *Report* and its *Summary.* The figure 52 for the number of cases is derived from the White Paper on the report (*op. cit.* n. 52); it represents the cases actually accepted by the government as involved in corrupt dealings.

62. Armah published a book called *Africa's Golden Road,* an ironically appropriate title in view of his spending record at the London High Commission and his later activities as minister of foreign trade.

63. *Report, 1965–66,* p. 23, para. 149. For pointed criticisms in Parliament of the state farms, see Ghana, *Parliamentary Debates,* vol. 38, no. 2 (14 January 1965), cols. 49–51, 60–65, 69–71; vol. 38, no. 3 (15 January 1965), cols. 100, 110; vol. 38, no. 13 (29 January 1965), cols. 498–501, 501–2, 503–7, 510–16, 516–19, 526, 528,; vol. 38, no. 14 (1 February 1965), cols. 556, 556–60, 566–69.)

64. *Reports, 1965–66,* p. 25, para. 160.

65. *Ibid.,* p. 40, para. 237, 238.

66. See, for example, the newspaper accounts of the coup in *New York Times,* February 26, 1966, pp. 1, 12; and *St. Louis Post-Dispatch,* February 24, 1966, p. 1. The argument is also made by Maj.-Gen. Albert K. Ocran in his book on the coup, *A Myth Is Broken* (London: Longmans, Green, 1968), pp. 19–21.

67. For details, see *Statement by the Government on the Report of the Commission Appointed to Enquire into the Matters Disclosed at the Trial of Captain Benjamin Awaithey Before a Court-Martial, and the Surrounding Circumstances,* White Paper no. 10/59 (Accra, 1959).

68. These charges are enumerated in a book Nkrumah wrote after the coup: *Dark Days in Ghana* (New York: International Publishers,

1968). He repeated them, in less detail, in a series of broadcasts to Ghana over Radio Conakry's "Voice of the African Revolution" during April and May 1966.

69. One F. A. Nzeribe, a Nigerian-born businessman operating in Ghana, had collected at least 30,000 new cedis (about $28,800) from certain expatriate firms for the alleged purpose of "conducting an opinion poll" on Ankrah's prospects for the forthcoming presidential election. Nzeribe admitted collecting the money, and said he had turned it over to Ankrah after deducting his agreed commission. *Ghanaian Times* (Accra), 3 May 1969, p. 1. Nzeribe was deported, and J. E. O. Nunoo (an NLC Police officer) was dismissed from the NLC in the aftermath of the affair. There are unsubstantiated reports that Ankrah did not consider that he had done anything wrong, and that he agreed to resign during a stormy NLC session only after Afrifa threatened to shoot him if he did not.

70. *Pioneer* (Kumasi), 21 June 1972, p. 1. There was in 1973 some indication that the NRC was looking into allegations that Busia had illegally exchanged over N₵1 million into sterling through an expatriate company in Accra.

71. The house in question drew sharp criticism in the only opposition newspaper still in operation in 1971, *The Spokesman*, edited by Kofi Badu, a former "Socialist boy" in favor during the Nkrumah period. Badu incurred a good deal of harassment, both legal and personal, for his criticisms of the Busia regime. See *The Spokesman*, 8, 11, 18 June 1971 (vol. 2, nos. 14, 15, and 17). Badu alleged that the Busia's house would cost at least $500,000; when Busia claimed it would cost only $155,000 (of which only $25,000 would come from public funds), Badu published a clearly tongue-in-cheek retraction. I talked with some people at the British construction firm A. Lang, which was contracting the job, and was told the true figure was closer to $300,000, of which perhaps a third came from public sources. For Busia's reply, see *Pioneer* 15 May 1971, pp. 1, 4.

72. See testimony of J. W. K. Harlley, former member of the NLC and later of the Presidential Commission, before Taylor Assets Committee, 22 June 1972. *Pioneer*, 23 June 1972, p. 1. Harlley, citing a receipt issued at the border, gave the contents of the portmanteau as "981 cedis, 57,960 American dollars, and 500 British pounds." The story of the portmanteau full of money was further corroborated by Joe Appiah, president of the Ghana Bar Association; *Pioneer*, 6 July

1972, p. 3. During my two years in Ghana the story came to me several times, though the amount cited each time differed from that stated by Harlley.

73. *Pioneer*, 1 June 1972, p. 1.

74. *Ibid.*, 4 May 1972, p. 1.

75. For details of the allegations against Da Rocha made by Kofi Badu, see *The Spokesman*, 5, 8, 23 January and 4 February 1971 (vol. 1, nos. 64, 65, 69, 71).

76. *Report ... Local Authorities and Educational Institutions, 1967–68, 1968–69.* The totals and percentages are my own, derived from figures and statements in the report.

77. *Report ... Public Boards and Corporations, 1967–68, 1968–69.* The total and percentages are my own, derived from figures and statements in the report. Some of the figures (including one erroneously cited) are reproduced under the title "The Character of the Ghanaian Elite" in *Legon Observer*, 5 November 1971, pp. 19–20. A 1965 publication of the Ministry of Finance, *The Budget*, which details the financial position of 32 state corporations up to 1963, indicated (p. 2) that at the end of that year these bodies had incurred a net accumulated deficit of £ 13,876,284 ($38,853,595), which compares with my 1967–69 figures. If this official figure is anywhere near being accurate, then the conclusion is unavoidable that not much changed between 1963 and 1969, at least as far as the earning power of the public corporations and institutions was concerned. The other evidence, cited above, indicates that patterns of intra- and inter-institutional corruption also changed little save in the identities and relationships of those involved.

78. *Report ... Treasury Accounts, 1967–68, 1968–*69. The percentage is my own computation.

79. *See Ghanaian Times*, 15 May 1971, p. 2, "2 Policemen Face Extortion Charge,"; and *Daily Graphic*, 16 May 1971, p. 1, "2 Policemen on Extortion Charges," for accounts of two separate incidents. In the former incident, the policemen asked a tradeswoman for N₡200 to avoid her arrest for selling contraband goods; in the latter, the policemen allegedly extorted N₡80 from a driver employed by the Volta River Authority "in order not to take action against him for failing to report an accident."

80. A few representative headlines culled from the Ghanaian press

during the Spring of 1971: "P.P. Won't Condone Bribery—Minister," *Ghanaian Times*, 26 February, p. 9; "Editorial: Checking the Embezzlers," *Pioneer* 10 April, p. 2; "Corruption Is National Enemy—Says Ewusie," *Ghanaian Times*, 5 April, p. 5; "Chiefs to Help Fight Corruption," *Pioneer*, 7 May, pp. 1, 4.

81. The sale of official forms extended to military recruiters; a steward who was employed by one of my colleagues at the University of Ghana was reportedly charged N₵50 for application forms to enter the Army. The last-listed item, a relatively common practice, received considerable publicity when, on 30 May, 1971, Minister of Rural Development and Social Welfare A. A. Munufie himself stopped a Ministry of Agriculture truck used as a "mammy wagon" (a truck used to transport passengers) and had the driver arrested. *Ghanaian Times*, 31 May 1971, p. 1.

82. This practice was common at the University of Ghana Post Office; it came to light when a number of university staff members complained that their letters were not being delivered (particularly letters overseas, which bore stamps of larger denominations), and an investigation was launched.

83. *Ghanaian Times*, 5 April 1971, p. 5. Dr. Ewusie, dean of the Faculty of Science, University College, Cape Coast, was speaking on the theme "the disciplined public servant," at a seminar sponsored by Ghana's Centre for Civic Education, one of whose campaigns was public education on the vices of corruption.

3: The Culture of Political Corruption: Supportive Values

1. For a discussion of concepts associated with efficacy, political competence, and civic competence, see Gabriel A. Almond and Sidney Verba, *The Civic Culture* (Princeton, N.J.: Princeton University Press, 1963), pp. 180–84. Applications of these concepts are discussed in the same work, pp. 184–257 *passim*.

2. Lloyd Fallers, *Bantu Bureaucracy* (Chicago: University of Chicago Press, 1965).

3. A Ghanaian political scientist, F. K. Drah, argues that this view has traditional roots. In support of this contention, he cites the example of "destoolment" (divestiture) of chiefs:

Whaf is not in doubt . . . is the fact that if and when a chief was destooled or "overthrown", the whole of his lineage was involved in his downfall. Those of them who happened to be stool office-holders were not seldom stripped of their offices *and* their titles, resulting in a whole redistribution of power. Extreme punitive and vindictive measures against the members of a defeated royal lineage were not uncommon: "You lose, I win and I take all." Without a scintilla of exaggeration, this "zero-sum" view of politics has been a powerful undercurrent of Ghanaian politics—at both the local and the central levels—up to the present. It was no new practice to, and was not initiated by, the C.P.P. nationalists and rulers.

"Political Tradition and the Search for Constitutional Democracy in Ghana: A Prolegomenon," *Ghana Journal of Sociology* 6, no. 1 (February 1970):10.

4. A conspicuous case in point is that of Mr. Kwabena Owusu, who in 1961 was named acting manager of the Ghana Distilleries Corporation. Mr. Owusu objected to the inflated prices charged by a London firm—Duncan, Gilbey, and Matheson—which was then paying kickbacks to NADECO; as a consequence, he and members of his family were arrested and humiliated, and he was finally dismissed from his position in January 1962. (Azu Crabbe Commission, pp. 43–44.) In the kingdom of the corrupt the honest man could hardly get near the throne, much less become king; the usual fate of one who refused to become corrupt was to be made an outcast, or suffer other social and economic penalties. Ayi Kwei Armah's vivid novel about corruption in Nkrumah's Ghana, *The Beautyful Ones Are Not Yet Born* (New York: Colliers-Macmillan, 1969), makes this point with great force.

5. Margaret J. Field, *Search for Security: An Ethno-psychiatric Study of Rural Ghana* (London: Faber and Faber, 1960), p. 26.

6. *Ibid.*

7. Maxwell Owusu, *Uses and Abuses of Political Power: A Case Study of Continuity and Change in the Politics of Ghana.* (Chicago: University of Chicago Press, 1970), p. 325.

8. *Ibid.*, p. 326.

9. *Ibid.*, p. 248.

10. Ghana, *Parliamentary Debates, Official Report*, Second Series, vol. 5, no. 4 (13 November 1970), col. 107.

11. *Ibid.*, vol. 6, no. 9 (8 March 1971), col. 300.

12. *Ibid.*, col. 301.

4: The Anatomy of Corruption

1. Steven J. Staats, "Corruption in the Soviet System," *Problems of Communism* 21, no. 1 (January-February 1972):42.

2. *Ibid.*

3. See p. 55 for an explanation.

4. Dr. Lewis Gann was kind enough to bring to my attention an apt similarity between the "verandah boys" of Ghana and the seventeenth-century Frenchmen (*fidèles*) who attached themselves to a "protector" or patron, giving him their devotion and allegiance, fighting for him, speaking, writing or intriguing for him, even on occasion going to prison or killing on his behalf, all in exchange for which (as Roland Mousnier put it) "the 'protector' clothes and feeds them, trusts them and takes them into his confidence, promotes their worldly advancement, arranges marriage for them, secures appointments for them, protects them, gets them out of prison." *Peasant Uprisings in Seventeenth-Century France, Russia, and China* (New York: Harper and Rowe Torchbooks, 1970), pp. 24–25. While the "verandah boys'" repertory of obligations did not include killing or going to prison, their relationship to their patrons certainly resembled that of the *fidèles* in the kinds of reciprocities involved and in the fact that both groups tended to grow or diminish in strength as the fortunes of the patrons waxed or waned.

5. Following each set of interviews, the respondents were given a typescript of the author's notes for the interviews, including those parts of the conversations which were quoted directly. The respondents could—and frequently did—excise any reference they felt could identify them. They also could stipulate which quotations might stand, which had to be removed, and which could be used as part of the narrative but without quotation marks.

6. My analysis in this section is in part derived from J. A. Barnes, "Networks and Political Process," in Marc J. Swartz, ed., *Local-Level Politics* (Chicago: Aldine, 1968), pp. 107–30. "Primary zone" is developed on pp. 113–14. Density, in Barnes's analysis (pp. 115–18)

refers to a proportion of actual links to the total possible number of links between persons in a defined zone. "We define this measure, the density of the zone, to be the proportion of the theoretically possible links that exist in fact" (p. 117). My use of "density" is to indicate only a proportion of links with "Alpha," the "primary star" (Barnes's term) in any cluster. In figure 5, *A* is the "primary star." My use of the term "cluster" is similar to Barnes's use of the term (p. 118) as an "egocentric zone," save that I use as a prime definition what appear to be functional distinctions used by the respondents to identify groups of people with which they related.

A caveat and a reminder must also be made at this point. I have examined the case of Mr. A. in considerable detail and used a variant of network analysis in my discussion not because such an analysis may be useful in assessing the volume of corruption in a sector of the polity, but because it illustrates the processual model developed earlier. The question of volume, quantity, and cash value of corrupt transactions is another matter entirely. A single transaction may involve diversion of very large sums of money, while repeated favors to subordinates, friends, clients, and relatives may divert only very small amounts. But that, again, is not the focus of this particular analysis. The question of volume and worth becomes important when the problems of consequences and systemic impact are considered. I broach these latter concerns in Chapters 5 and 6.

7. This is an old bureaucratic distinction. Officials in "line" positions deal directly with the public; those in "staff" jobs do so rarely or not at all. For example, window clerks and letter carriers of the U.S. Postal Service are "line" officials; letter sorters, truck drivers, accountants, post-office managers, and the like occupy "staff" positions, since they deal primarily with fellow postal employees. It need hardly be added that the distinction often becomes blurred in practice, but it remains useful for our analysis.

8. *White Paper on the Report of the Jiagge Commission of Inquiry into the Assets of Specified Persons*, White Paper no. 3/69 (Accra, 1969). The amounts noted are either as given by the White Paper or translated from amounts given in Ghanaian pounds (G £1 = N₵2.10).

9. Mr. Richard Rathbone of the School of Oriental and African Studies, University of London, kindly permitted the use of a

mimeographed set of his notes entitled "Convention People's Party Politicians: Results of the Military Government's Inquiries." The quotation is from page 2 of the notes.

10. See chapter 2, n. 39.

11. Jiagge Commission, p. 73. Emphasis added.

12. Rathbone, "CPP Politicians," p. 1.

13. *Ibid.*

14. The committee held 338 sittings and examined thirty-one witnesses, as well as the Authority's accounts and internal records. Its report was published in 1971 as the *Report of the Committee of Enquiry on the Erstwhile Football Pools Authority*, P.V. Osei-Hwere, Chairman [Osei-Hwere Committee] (Accra, 1971). It encompasses 218 legal-sized mimeographed pages, and includes not only the detailed findings of the committee, but eleven appendixes containing audit reports, earnings tabulations, and certain relevant correspondence. With the possible exception of the Ollenu Commission report (Import Licenses), it is the most detailed of the post-coup inquiry reports. The government's White Paper on the report (WP no. 1/71) also was published in 1971.

15. Before 1961, the main pools firms operating in Ghana (Zetter's, Vernon's, Cope's, Victory International, Soccer Pools, Littlewood's, Empire) had their own agents in the country who distributed the tickets (printed in England), collected the stakes, and forwarded the coupons directly to Britain. Winners were mailed sterling checks directly from the United Kingdom. After 1966, Ghanaian football pools were based on local (Ghanaian) matches, and the whole system came under stringent supervision and control.

(I am grateful to Dr. Michael Parkinson, whose patient explanations provided the basis for the above summary and for the other description of the pools system included in the text.)

16. Osei-Hwere Committee, pp. 4–7.

17. This is an estimate, based on two audits and a projection. Commissions during 1961–62 totaled £ 130,648 (*Report*, p. 121); during 1962–63, they amounted to £ 133,488 (*Report*, p. 193). The gross take estimate is my own extrapolation from the account in the report.

18. *Report*, p. 106, para. 411. Kanbi's activities are noted on pp. 4–5. It should be added that F. K. D. Goka became minister of finance

in 1961 following the resignation of Komlah Gbedemah. Goka had been minister of trade; his shift was one of the consequences of the "Dawn Broadcast" reorganization.

19. *Ibid.,* p. 48, para. 135.

20. *Ibid.,* pp. 55–63, paras. 176–213. The quotation is on p. 60 (para. 197).

21. *Ibid.,* p. 56, para. 183.

22. F. G. Bailey, "Parapolitical Systems," in Marc. J. Swartz, ed., *Local-Level Politics* (Chicago: Aldine, 1968), p. 281.

23. Maxwell Owusu, *Uses and Abuses of Political Power: A Case Study of Continuity and Change in the Politics of Ghana* (Chicago: University of Chicago Press, 1970).

24. An analysis that reflects this pluralist view is Sanjeeva Nayak, "An Analytical Model of Hegemonial Tension among Ghanaian Elites (1957–1966)," an unpublished paper presented to the 1970 Munich World Congress of the International Political Science Association.

25. Bob Fitch and Mary Oppenheimer, "Ghana: End of an Illusion," *Monthly Review* 18, no. 3 (July-August 1966):107.

26. Maxwell Owusu comes to a similar conclusion in *Uses and Abuses of Political Power,* p. 326: "The political party (CPP) in fact became the single most powerful group in Ghanaian society, for, once it had become the government, it exploited all the power available to a national government in relation to the control, possession, and distribution of almost all the resources in the country. Membership in the dominant, and since 1964, the only party, therefore became one of the best means to power, wealth, and certainly high social status."

Owusu completes the last sentence, above, in a footnote on the same page: "Particularly for those who either had no other avenue to wealth or who strongly felt relative economic deprivation."

27. Dennis Austin, *Politics in Ghana 1946–60* (New York: Oxford University Press, 1964), p. 404.

28. *Ghana: End of an Illusion,* p. 107.

29. This is Nkrumah's own formula, quoted from his "Dawn Broadcast," 8 April 1961.

30. For confirmation, see, for example, the *Interim and Final Reports of the Commission of Inquiry into the Accra-Tema City Coun-*

cil [Accra-Tema Commission] (Accra, 1969); *Report of the Commission Appointed under Act 250 to Enquire into the Affairs of the Sekondi-Takoradi City Council* [Gaisie Commission] (Accra, 1970); and *Report of the Committee to Enquire into the Allocation of the Keta Market Stalls and other Ancillary Matters* [Keta Committee], (Accra, 1969).

31. Adamafio himself fell from power in 1963 following the Kulungugu incident, in which a bomb was thrown at Nkrumah. For details of the 1961–63 intraparty conflicts, see Austin, *Politics in Ghana*, pp. 402–14.

32. Henry Bretton, *The Rise and Fall of Kwame Nkrumah* (New York, 1966), p. 106.

33. *Report of the Commission of Inquiry into the Circumstances Surrounding the Establishment of the Ghana Cargo Handling Company* [Korantang-Addow Commission] (Accra, 1967), p. 47.

34. Azu Crabbe Commission, pp. 23–24.

5: Causes and Consequences

1. *Comparative Political Corruption* (Englewood Cliffs, N.J.: Prentice-Hall, 1972), p. ix.

2. (Singapore: Donald Moore Press, 1968), p. iii. Alatas's book is subtitled *The Nature, Function, Causes and Prevention of Corruption.* Lasswell is co-author, with Arnold A. Rogow, of *Power, Corruption, and Rectitude* (Englewood Cliffs, N.J.: Prentice-Hall, 1963).

3. Alatas, *The Sociology of Corruption*, pp. 7–9. Alatas's references are: Wang An-shih, "'Memorial of a Myriad Words' (Wan Yen Shu)," in H. R. Williamson, *Wang An Shih*, vol. 2 (London: A. Probsthain, 1935); Ibn Khaldun, *The Muqaddimah*, vols. 1–3, tr. F. Rosenthal (London: Routledge-Kegan Paul, 1958). "Vol. 2 [of Khaldun] is of special interest," notes Alatas.

4. *Report of the Committee on the Prevention of Corruption* (the "Santhanam Report"). (New Delhi: Ministry of Home Affairs, 1964).

5. J. A. G. Mackie, "The Commission of Four Report on Corruption," *Bulletin of Indonesian Economic Studies* 6, no. 3 (November 1970):87–101. I am indebted for this citation to Wyn N. Hoadley, whose paper "Political Corruption in Developing Countries: Three

Approaches" (presented in 1972 to the Australasian Political Science Association Conference), deals substantially with Indonesian corruption.

6. Some of the relevant Ghanaian legislation is as follows:

The Criminal Code (Amendment) Act—1/3/62 (Act 108)
The Criminal Code (Amendment) Act—3/1/63 (Act 157)
The Criminal Procedure Code (Amendment) Act—9/2/65 (Act 261)
The Public Property (Prevention) and Corrupt Practices Act—12/6/62 (Act 121)
The Corrupt Practices (Prevention) Act—3/3/64 Act 230)
The Commissions of Inquiry Act, 1964 (Act 250)

Of the post-coup Commissions of Inquiry, only two, the Apaloo and Ollenu commissions, were appointed under Act 230; the remainder were appointed under Act 250 or under other NLC or Second Republic decrees and legislation. The civil service statutes and regulations excerpted in Appendix B (see pp. 121–23) must be added to this list.

7. *The Beautyful Ones Are Not Yet Born* (London, 1969), p. 180. Kwei Armah's reference is probably to the Abraham Commission. "Legon" refers to the University of Ghana at Legon, a suburb of Accra.

8. I have undoubtedly committed some distortion in summing up this complicated problem in such simple terms. For an accessibly clear discussion of causality in the social sciences see Robert Dubin, *Theory-Building* (New York: The Free Press, 1969), pp. 89–107.

9. Arnold J. Heidenheimer, ed., *Political Corruption* (New York, 1970), p. 18.

10. Colin Leys, "What Is the Problem about Corruption," *Journal of Modern African Studies* 3, no. 2 (1965), cited in Heidenheimer, *Political Corruption*, pp. 19 and 37. Heidenheimer, whose perspective is comparative and cross-national, proposes another, "more modest" form of Leys's question: "Which of the various forms of behavior that a significant portion of the population regards as corrupt are more likely to be more pervasive in one society than another, and why?" (p. 37).

11. M. McMullan, "A Theory of Corruption," *Sociological Review* 9, no. 2 (June 1961):181–200; and Ronald Wraith and Edgar

Simpkins, *Corruption in Developing Countries* (New York: W. W. Norton, 1964), pp. 33–45. Both of these selections are reprinted in Heidenheimer, pp. 317–30 and 331–40, respectively. See also Ebow Mends, "Traditional Values and Bribery and Corruption," *Legon Observer* 5, no. 25 (4 December 1970):13–14.

Mends expresses this conclusion in the strongest terms: "It would seem ... that in no direct way could it be held that bribery and corruption have their roots in customs and usages" (p. 14).

12. Kofi A. Busia, *The Position of the Chief in the Modern Political System of Ashanti* (London: Oxford University Press, 1951), p. 50. Everything a man possessed—gold dust, wives, slaves, farms—became stool property when he became a chief. Thus, when a chief who abused stool property was subject to "destoolment," it meant not only deposition but loss of all his worldly wealth.

13. Busia alludes to various abuses of trust by chiefs and officials in *ibid.* For a detailed account of a long and often violent dispute over succession, see J. A. Braimah and Jack Goody, *Salaga: The Struggle for Power* (London: Longmans, 1967); see also Goody's comments in his "Circulating Succession among the Gonja," in Jack Goody, ed., *Succession to High Office* (London: Cambridge University Press, 1966). Even more to the point is R. S. Rattray, *Ashanti Law and the Constitution* (London: Oxford University Press, 1956), which details various sanctions that could be applied against officials and chiefs who committed acts tantamount to abuse or misuse of political goods.

14. In a citation of the relevant literature concerning traditional Ghanaian societies, the works by Busia, Rattray, Braimah, and Goody (noted above) are a beginning. Other important studies include Annor Adjaye, *Nzima Land* (London: Headley Bros., 1931); A. W. Cardinall, *The Natives of the Northern Territories of the Gold Coast* (London: George Routledge and Sons, 1920); M. J. Field, *Social Organization of the Ga People* (London: Crown Agents, 1940); Caseley Hayford, *Gold Coast Native Institutions* (London: Sweet and Maxwell, 1903); M. Manoukian, *The Ewe-Speaking People of Togoland and the Gold Coast* (London: Oxford University Press, 1952); John Mensah Sarbah, *Fanti National Constitution* (London: William Clowes and Sons, 1906); Charles W. Welman, *The Native States of the Gold Coast*, vols. 1 and 2 (London: Crown Agents, 1930).

A useful recent study with wider focus is Robert L. Tignor, "Colonial Chiefs in Chiefless Societies," *Journal of Modern African*

Studies 9, no. 3 (1971):339–59. Tignor's comments on traditional zero-sum politics are particularly interesting.

15. Testimony to the survival of such practices was provided in 1971 by a Ghanaian government back-bencher, Mr. I. K. Osei-Duah. Arguing that traditional authorities should keep proper accounts and treasuries, he cited two examples of questionable appropriation of moneys:

> I cannot imagine how a traditional authority could use N₵ 12,000 and term it as legal expenses; and pay out N₵ 7,476 and term it "Paid to prominent persons in accordance with custom.". . . . I can also cite the case where, without the consent of the citizens, the traditional authority decided on their own to appropriate N₵ 3,000 to themselves. At the same time, it treated this money as legal administrative expense. I am sure this traditional authority has got an office. It has not got a treasurer, it has not even got a messenger. Yet it says: "Administrative expenses." What administrative expenses?

Republic of Ghana, *Parliamentary Debates, Official Report*, Second Series, vol. 6, no. 10 (Tuesday, 9 March 1971), column 328. See also Busia, *op. cit.*, pp. 199–208; Busia also discusses the bribery of stool electors, pp. 209–14.

16. William Ofori Atta, the foreign minister in Dr. Busia's cabinet, summed up this attitude in these terms: "There was a time when we regarded the government as a foreign Government, and therefore some people, in their own circles, even regarded it as a patriotic duty if they were able to steal from the government." *Parliamentary Debates, op. cit.* n. 15, column 313.

17. Victor T. Le Vine, *Political Corruption and the Informal Polity* (Inaugural Lecture, 4 February 1971, University of Ghana, Legon) (Legon: University of Ghana Press, 1971), pp. 16–17.

18. Lord Hailey, for example, notes: "A Colonial Office Conference on African Administration held in 1947 expressed views which seemed to point to the progressive replacement of the Native Authority system by institutions following the patterns of Local Government bodies in Great Britain." Lord [William M. H.] Hailey, *An African Survey*, rev. ed. (New York: Oxford University Press, 1957), p. 204; see also Hailey's comments at pp. 200–2.

19. Francis Kofi Drah, "Some Thoughts on Freedom in a Post-

Colonial African Setting," *Economic Bulletin of Ghana* 12, no. 1 (1968): 41. Drah's description derives in part from Dennis Austin, *Politics in Ghana, 1946–60* (London: Oxford University Press, 1964), pp. 13–28. See also W. Arthur Lewis's description of the "disaffected young people," in his *Politics in West Africa* (London: Allen and Unwin, 1965), pp. 21–23.

20. Ali A. Mazrui, "Social Distance and the Transclass Man," pp. 147–59 in his *Cultural Engineering and Nation-Building in East Africa* (Evanston, Ill.: Northwestern University Press, 1972).

21. Jitendra Mohan, "Nkrumah and Nkrumaism," in Ralph Milbrand and John Saville, eds., *The Socialist Register 1967* (London: Merlin Press, 1967), pp. 191–228. Mohan's study is one of the most perceptive ever written on the rise of Nkrumah, seen in the perspective of the social and political changes that took place in Ghana after 1945. The discussion in this subsection owes much to his trenchant analysis.

22. *Ibid.*, p. 194.

23. Drah, "Some Thoughts on Freedom," pp. 42–43. See also Austin, *Politics in Ghana*, pp. 42–44.

24. Mazrui, "Social Distance . . . ," *loc. cit.* n. 20, p. 147. See also Mazrui's "The Monarchical Tendency in African Political Culture," *British Journal of Sociology* 18, no. 3 (September 1967):231–50, reprinted in Mazrui, *Violence and Thought: Essays on Social Tensions in Africa* (London: Longmans, 1969), pp. 206–30.

25. Mohan, "Nkrumah and Nkrumaism," *loc. cit.*, p. 208.

26. *Ibid.*, p. 212.

27. The percentage data are from Walter Birmingham, I. Neustadt, and E. N. Omaboe, eds., *A Study of Contemporary Ghana, Volume One: The Economy of Ghana* (London: Allen and Unwin, 1966), pp. 124–25. The other figures are from Ghana, Office of Government Statistics, *Labour Statistics, 1959*, p. 4. The 1950 figure is 77,375.

28. Ghana, Budget Secretariat, *Financial Statement, 1961–62*, p. 27; Ghana, *Annual Estimates, 1961–62, Part I*. The 53 percent is my own computation.

29. Elliot J. Berg, "Structural Transformation versus Gradualism: Recent Economic Development in Ghana and the Ivory Coast," in Philip Foster and Aristide R. Zolberg, eds., *Ghana and the Ivory*

Coast: Perspectives on Modernization (Chicago: University of Chicago Press, 1971), p. 211.

30. This characterization of the Ghanaian colonial service is adapted from a description of the Nigerian colonial service provided by J. Donald Kingsley in his essay, "Bureaucracy and Political Development, with Particular Reference to Nigeria," in Joseph La Palombara, ed., *Bureaucracy and Political Development* (Princeton, N.J.: Princeton University Press, 1963), p. 307. I use it because it seems, *mutatis mutandis*, to apply to the Gold Coast as well.

31. Parts of these speeches are quoted directly; other parts are summarized by Nkrumah in his *I Speak of Freedom* (New York: Praeger, 1961). For the 1956 speech, see pp. 71–84; the 1959 speech is quoted and discussed in pp. 169–74. My quotation is at p. 173.

32. Robert E. Dowse, *Modernization in Ghana and the U.S.S.R.* (London: Routledge-Kegan Paul, 1969), p. 57.

33. David E. Apter, "Ghana," in James S. Coleman and Carl G. Rosberg, Jr., eds., *Political Parties and National Integration in Tropical Africa* (Berkeley: University of California Press, 1964), pp. 313–14. Apter quotes from a newspaper attack that preceded the reorganizations: the government-owned *Evening News* called civil servants "intellectual spivs" and the Civil Service Commission a "semi-colonial" agency. It also argued that "the appointment of anti-party, anti-socialist rascals on the basis of bourgeois qualifications leaves open the possibilities of creating so many agents of neo-colonialism in a state administration."

The reorganization was part of the more general move to centralize power in Flagstaff House—i.e., the President's Office. During 1964 the party, the various cabinet departments, the Trades Union Congress, and the State Enterprises Secretariat (responsible for supervision of the many statutory corporations and enterprises) all came to operate directly out of Flagstaff House. By mid-1965, the Office of the Planning Commission, already under the President (and nominally responsible to the State Planning Commission), had become firmly lodged in Flagstaff House as well. Bretton, in *The Rise and Fall of Kwame Nkrumah* (New York, 1966), correctly describes the new situation: "The President's Office and Flagstaff House resembled a market place where presidential fiat was traded—genuinely presidential or just assumed or alleged—or where it was altered or adjusted."

(p. 113). The Bank of Ghana, by statute an independent body, also eventually came under the control of Nkrumah's cronies, and was used as an instrument of political pressure or reward, particularly in connection with foreign exchange dealings.

34. Bretton, *The Rise and Fall of Kwame Nkrumah*, pp. 117–18.

35. Austin, *Politics in Ghana*, p. 158.

36. Berg, "Structural Transformation versus Gradualism," *loc. cit.*, p. 197.

37. Much of the discussion in this section is drawn from Berg's incisive analysis, *ibid.*, pp. 210–14.

38. *Ibid.*, p. 210. It has been suggested to me that Berg's description seems also to fit the U.S. federal establishment in the wake of the Watergate affair.

39. The relationship between structural fragmentation and the growth of political corruption is well established in the literature on corruption. A recent work on organized crime and corruption in America, for example, forcefully makes the connection: John A. Gardiner, *The Politics of Corruption: Organized Crime in an American City* (New York: Russell Sage Foundation, 1970).

40. Heidenheimer, *Political Corruption*, pp. 479–86.

41. Joseph S. Nye, "Corruption and Political Development: A Cost-Benefit Analysis," *American Political Science Review* 61, no. 2 (June 1967):417–27; abridged in Heidenheimer, *Political Corruption*, pp. 564–78.

42. Wyn N. Hoadley, a new Zealand political scientist, has already attempted to apply Nye's scheme to a study of Indonesia. See Hoadley, *op. cit.* n.5.

43. Heidenheimer, *Political Corruption*, p. 484.

44. Nye, in Heidenheimer, *Political Corruption*, p. 573.

45. No one would fault the military regime of the National Redemption Council, for want of effort to eliminate or check political corruption. In February 1973, a little more than a year after the NRC took power, military tribunals began trying employees of the Produce Buying Agency, a branch of the Cocoa Marketing Board, on charges of embezzlement and misappropriation of cocoa funds. From 1966 to 1972, it was reported, misappropriations, frauds, and embezzlements in the cocoa trade amounted to nearly N₵ 60 million (about $55 million). *West Africa*, 12 February 1973, p. 215.

46. Nye, "Corruption and Political Development," pp. 421–23 (reference is to original article).

47. The phrases are from Reginald H. Green, "Reflections on Economic Strategy, Structure, Implementation and Necessity: Ghana and the Ivory Coast, 1957–67," in Foster and Zolberg, *Ghana and the Ivory Coast*, pp. 251–60. Green was engaged in teaching and research in West Africa and Ghana between 1960 and 1965; it is probable he had a hand in preparing Nkrumah's *Neo-Colonialism, the Last Stage of Imperialism* (London: Thomas Nelson and Sons, 1965).

48. Jon Woronoff, *West African Wager* (Metuchen, N.J.: Scarecrow Press, 1972), p. 192. It should be added that the steel plant had serious difficulties obtaining scrap, and the atomic reactor project (at Kwabenya, near the University of Ghana) was abandoned following the coup in 1966, with much of the equipment left to rust at Tema. Some 300 employees of the Ghana Atomic Energy Commission were retained on the job, however, and continued to occupy quarters and draw salaries and perquisities through 1971. The reactor was a Russian venture, and much of the cost (about $10.8 million) was met by Soviet credits and grants.

49. Herbert H. Werlin notes that in Ghana "corruption is seen as intensifying inter-ethnic conflict." Corruption can foster ethnic discrimination, which in turn can lead to still more corruption. Thus as Nkrumah became more insecure, he became increasingly concerned with the tribal origins of civil servants and high party functionaries and surrounded himself with Nzimas (his own ethnic group). Other members of the ruling elite, following their leader's example, put their own tribesmen into strategic positions of power and authority "in order to settle old scores and/or to buttress their own positions in the top-most institutions of the state." Werlin, "The Consequences of Corruption: The Ghanaian Experience," *Political Science Quarterly* 88, no. 1 (March 1973):82.

6: Ghanaian Political Corruption in Perspective

1. Some of the observations that follow are paraphrased from the author's letter to *Africa* (Paris), no. 10 (June 1972):9.

2. For details, see David Goldsworthy, "Ghana's Second Republic; A Post-Mortem," *African Affairs* 72, no. 286 (January 1973): 8–25.

3. Stanislas Andreski, *The African Predicament* (New York: Atherton, 1968), pp. 92–109.

4. John Waterbury, "Endemic and Planned Corruption in a Monarchical Regime," *World Politics* 25, no. 4 (July 1973):555.

5. This is not to imply that any qualified observer of Morocco's political or economic scene predicts the *imminent* collapse of King Hassan's regime. Such authorities, however, are nearly unaminous in pointing to a range of problems that might seriously undermine the regime if they remain unresolved: official corruption, the decline and mismanagement of the economy, official repression, discontent among students and younger elements of the military. Waterbury implies as much in his article, and similar views are expressed by Samir Amin in his *The Maghreb in the Modern World* (Baltimore: Penguin Books, 1970), particularly pp. 186–87; and by Mark I. Cohen and Lorna Hahn, *Morocco: Old Land, New Nation* (New York: Praeger, 1969), pp. 274–75. There are other reasons for lack of confidence in the long-range prospects of King Hassan's regime: the King narrowly escaped assassination in July 1971, when his palace was attacked and overrun by cadets from the military school; and in August 1972 his personal Boeing 727 (with him aboard) was attacked by Moroccan air force jets and almost shot down. A casualty of the latter incident was General Mohammed Oufkir, Hassan's minister of Defense, who reportedly committed suicide because he was implicated in the plot to kill the King. Ironically, Oufkir was instrumental in frustrating the 1971 attempt on the King's life.

6. *New York Times*, January 22, 1973, p. 12.

7. James O'Connell, "The Inevitability of Instability," *Journal of Modern African Studies* 5, no. 2 (September 1967):181.

8. *Ibid.*

9. *Ibid.*, p. 182.

10. *Ibid.*, p. 187.

11. *Ibid.*, p. 188.

12. Goldsworthy, "Ghana's Second Republic," *passim.*

13. O'Connell, "The Inevitability of Instability," p. 189.

14. *Ibid.*

Bibliography

This bibliography includes only those books, articles, and other items cited in the text or notes of this study, or used in its preparation. For additional materials on corruption, the reader is directed to the bibliographies in the works by Heidenheimer and Scott, noted below.

1. Books and Articles

Almond, Gabriel A., and Powell, G. Bingham, Jr. *Comparative Politics: A Developmental Approach.* Boston: Little, Brown, 1966.

Almond, Gabriel A., and Verba, Sidney. *The Civic Culture.* Princeton, N.J.: Princeton University Press, 1963.

Alatas, Syed Hussein. *The Sociology of Corruption: The Nature, Function, Causes and Prevention of Corruption.* Singapore: Donald Moore Press, 1968.

Alexander, Herbert J. "Corrupt Practices." In *Encyclopedia Britannica,* 1971.

Andreski, Stanislas. *The African Predicament.* New York: Atherton, 1968.

Apter, David E. "Ghana." In James S. Coleman and Carl G. Rosberg Jr., eds. *Political Parties and National Integration in Tropical Africa,* pp. 313–14. Berkeley; University of California Press, 1964.

_____. *Ghana in Transition.* 2d ed. Princeton: Princeton University Press, 1972.

Armah, Ayi Kwei. *The Beautyful Ones Are Not Yet Born.* New York: Colliers-Macmillan, 1969.

_____. *Africa's Golden Road.* London: Heinemann, 1965.

Austin, Dennis. *Politics in Ghana, 1946-60.* New York and London Oxford University Press, 1964.

Barnes, John A. "Networks and Political Process." In Marc J. Swartz, ed., *Local-Level Politics,* pp. 107–30. Chicago: Aldine, 1968.

Bailey, F. G. "Parapolitical Systems." In Marc J. Swartz, ed., *Local-Level Politics*, pp. 281–94. Chicago : Aldine, 1968.

Berg, Elliot J. "Structural Transformation versus Gradualism; Recent Economic Development in Ghana and the Ivory Coast." In Philip Foster and Aristide R. Zolberg, eds., *Ghana and the Ivory Coast: Perspectives on Modernization*. Chicago: University of Chicago Press, 1971.

Bing, Geoffrey. *Reap the Whirlwind*. London: MacGibbon and Kee, 1968.

Birmingham, Walter; Neustadt, I.; and Omaboe, E. N., eds. *A Study of Contemporary Ghana*: vol. 1, *The Economy of Ghana*; vol. 2, *Some Aspects of Social Structure*. London: Allen and Unwin, 1966.

Braimah, J. A., and Goody, Jack. *Salaga: The Struggle for Power*. London: Longmans, 1967.

Bretton, Henry L. "The Overthrow of Kwame Nkrumah." In Andrew Gyorgy, Hubert S. Gibbs, and Robert S. Jordan, eds., *Problems in International Relations*. 3d ed., pp. 277–99. Englewood Cliffs, N.J.: Prentice-Hall, 1970.

—————. *The Rise and Fall of Kwame Nkrumah: A Study of Personal Rule in Africa*. New York: Frederick Praeger, 1966.

Busia, Kofi A. *The Position of the Chief in the Modern Political System of Ashanti*. New York and London: Oxford University Press, 1951.

Callaway, Barbara, and Card, Emily, "Political Constraints on Economic Development in Ghana." In Michael F. Lofchie, ed., *The State of the Nations: Constraints on Development in Independent Africa*, pp. 65–92. Berkeley: University of California Press, 1971.

Card, Emily. "Organizing for Mobilization: Voluntary Associations and Party Auxiliaries in Ghana." In Audrey C. Smock, ed., *Comparative Politics: A Reader in Institutionalization and Modernization*, pp. 292–327. Boston: Allyn and Bacon, 1973.

"Corruption in African Public Life." *Legon Observer* 1 (2 September 1966):6–8.

Dawson, Richard E., and Prewitt, Kenneth. *Political Socialization*. Boston: Little, Brown, 1969.

Dowse, Robert E. *Modernization in Ghana and the U.S.S.R.* London: Routledge and Kegan Paul, 1969.

Drah, Francis Kofi. "Political Tradition and the Search for Constitutional Democracy in Ghana: A Prolegomenon." *Ghana Journal of Sociology* 6, no. 1 (February 1970):1–19.

_____. "Some Thoughts on Freedom in a Post-Colonial African Setting." *Economic Bulletin of Ghana* 12, no. 1 (1968):41.

Fallers, Lloyd. *Bantu Bureaucracy.* Chicago: University of Chicago Press, 1965.

Field, Margaret J. *Search for Security: An Ethno-psychiatric Study of Rural Ghana.* London: Faber and Faber, 1960.

Finlay, David. "The Ghana Coup." Unpublished paper, 1966.

Fitch, Bob, and Oppenheimer, Mary. "Ghana: End of an Illusion." *Monthly Review* 18, no. 3 (July-August 1966). The entire issue is devoted to this study.

Folson, Kweku. "An African Tragedy." *Encounter* 33, no. 1 (July 1969):35–43.

Gardiner, John A. *The Politics of Corruption: Organized Crime in an American City.* New York: Russell Sage Foundation, 1970.

Genoud, Roger. *Nationalism and Economic Development in Ghana.* New York: Frederick Praeger, 1969.

Goldsworthy, David. "Ghana's Second Republic: A Post-Mortem." *African Affairs* 72, no. 286 (January 1973):8–25.

Goody, Jack, ed. *Succession to High Office.* London: Cambridge University Press, 1966.

Green, Reginald H. "Reflections on Economic Strategy, Structure, Implementation and Necessity: Ghana and the Ivory Coast." In Philip Foster and Aristide R. Zolberg, eds., *Ghana and the Ivory Coast: Perspectives on Modernization*, pp. 251–60. Chicago: University of Chicago Press, 1971.

Hailey, Lord William H. *An African Survey.* Rev. ed. New York: Oxford University Press, 1957.

Heidenheimer, Arnold J., ed. *Political Corruption.* New York: Holt, Rinehart and Winston, 1970.

Hoadley, Wyn N. "Political Corruption in Developing Countries: Three Approaches." Unpublished paper, presented to 1972 Australasian Political Science Association Conference, Wellington, N.Z.

Howell, Thomas A., and Jeffrey P. Rajasooria, eds., *Ghana & Nkrumah.* New York: Facts on File, Inc., 1972.

Ikoku, Samuel G. [pseud. Julius Sago]. *Le Ghana de Kwame Nkrumah.* Paris: François Maspéro, 1971.

Ilchman, Warren F., and Uphoff, Norman Thomas. *The Political Economy of Change*. Berkeley: University of California Press, 1969.

Jenkins, George. "An Informal Political Economy." In Jeffrey Butler and Alphonse A. Castagno, eds., *Boston University Papers on Africa*, pp. 166–194. New York: Frederick Praeger, 1970.

Kingsley, J. Donald. "Bureaucracy and Political Development, with Particular Reference to Nigeria." In Joseph La Palombara, ed., *Bureaucracy and Political Development*, pp. 601–18. Princeton, N.J.: Princeton University Press, 1963.

Kling, Merle. "Violence and Politics in Latin America." *The Sociological Review Monograph*, no. 11: "Latin-American Sociological Studies." University of Keele [Staffordshire, Eng.], February 1967, pp. 119–32.

Kraus, Jon. "Arms and Politics in Ghana." In Claude E. Welch, ed., *Soldier and State in Africa*, pp. 154–223. Evanston: Northwestern University Press, 1970.

————. "Political Change, Conflict and Development in Ghana." In Philip Foster and Aristide Zolberg, eds., *Ghana and the Ivory Coast: Perspectives on Modernization*, pp. 33–72. Chicago: University of Chicago Press, 1971.

LeVine, Victor T. "The Political Cultures of French-Speaking Africa." *Ghana Social Science Journal* 1, no. 2 (November 1971):63–79.

————. *Political Corruption and the Informal Polity*. Inaugural Lecture Series. Legon: University of Ghana Press, 1971.

Lewis, W. Arthur. *Politics in West Africa*. London: Allen and Unwin, 1965.

Leys, Colin. "What is the Problem about Corruption." *Journal of Modern African Studies* 3, no. 2 (1965):215–30.

Mackie, J. A. G. "The Commission of Four Report on Corruption." *Bulletin of Indonesian Economic Studies* 6, no. 3 (November 1970):87–100.

"Les Mauvais Draps." *Afrique Nouvelle*, 15–21 April 1962, p. 4.

Mazrui, Ali A. *Cultural Engineering and Nation-Building in East Africa*. Evanston, Ill.: Northwestern University Press, 1972.

————. "The Monarchical Tendency in African Political Culture." *British Journal of Sociology* 18, no. 3 (September 1967):231–50.

McMullan, M. "A Theory of Corruption." *Sociological Review* 9, no. 2 (June 1961):181–200.

Mends, Ebow. "Traditional Values and Bribery and Corruption." *Legon Observer* 5, no. 25 (4–17 December 1970):13–14.

Mohan, Jitendra. "Nkrumah and Nkrumaism." In Ralph Milbrand and John Saville, eds., *The Socialist Register 1967.* London: Merlin Press, 1967.

Mousnier, Roland. *Peasant Uprisings in Seventeenth-Century France, Russia, and China.* New York: Harper and Rowe, 1970.

Nayak, Sanjeeva. "An Analytical Model of Hegemonial Tension among Ghanaian Elites (1957–1966)." Unpublished paper presented to Seventh IPSA World Congress, Munich, 1970.

Nkrumah, Kwame. *Dark Days in Ghana.* New York: International Publishers, 1968.

_____. *I Speak of Freedom.* New York: Frederick Praeger, 1961.

_____. *Neo-Colonialism, the Last Stage of Imperialism.* London: Thomas Nelson and Sons, 1965.

Nye, Joseph S. "Corruption and Political Development: A Cost-Benefit Analysis." *American Political Science Review* 61, no. 2 (June 1967):417–27.

O'Connell, James. "The Inevitability of Instability." *Journal of Modern African Studies* 5, no. 2 (September, 1967):181–91.

Ocran, Maj.-Gen. Albert K. *A Myth Is Broken.* London: Longmans, Green, 1968.

Omari, T. Peter. *Kwame Nkrumah: The Anatomy of an African Dictatorship.* Accra: Moxon Paperbacks, 1970.

Ottenberg, Simon. "Local Government and the Law in Southern Nigeria." *Journal of Asian and African Studies* 2, nos. 1–2 (January and April 1967):12–26.

Owusu, Maxwell. *Uses and Abuses of Political Power: A Case Study of Continuity and Change in the Politics of Ghana.* Chicago: University of Chicago Press, 1970.

Pinkney, Robert. *Ghana Under Military Rule, 1966–69.* London: Methuen, 1972.

Pooley, Beverly J. "Corruption and Development in Ghana." Unpublished paper, 1969.

Rathbone, Richard. "Convention People's Party Politicians: Results of the Military Government's Inquiries." Unpublished notes. Mimeographed.

Rattray, Robert Sutherland. *Ashanti Law and Constitution*. London: Oxford University Press, 1956.

Ravenholt, Albert. "The Peso Price of Politics." *AUFS Reports, Southeast Asia Series*, no. 6 (May 1958):40.

Reitsch, Hanna. *Ich flog fur Kwame Nkrumah*. Munich: Lehman, 1968.

Scott, James C. *Comparative Political Corruption*. Englewood Cliffs, N.J.: Prentice-Hall, 1972.

Sharpston, M. J. "The Economics of Corruption," *New Society* (London), 26 November 1970, p. 944.

Sklar, Richard. "The Ordeal of Chief Awolowo." In Gwendolen M. Carter, ed., *Politics in Africa—7 Cases*, pp. 119-66. New York: Harcourt, Brace, and World, 1966.

Staats, Steven J. "Corruption in the Soviet System." *Problems of Communism* 21, no. 1 (January-February 1972):40-47

Thompson, W. Scott. *Ghana's Foreign Policy, 1957-1966*. Princeton, N.J.: Princeton University Press, 1969.

Tignor, Robert L. "Colonial Chiefs in Chiefless Societies." *Journal of Modern African Studies* 9, no. 3 (1971):339-59.

Uba, Sam. "Corruption in Africa." *Africa*, no. 8 (April 1972):16-17.

Waterbury, John. "Endemic and Planned Corruption in a Monarchical Regime." *World Politics* 25, no. 4 (July 1973):533-55

Werlin, Herbert, "The Consequences of Corruption: The Ghanaian Experience." *Political Science Quarterly* 88, no. 1 (March 1973):71-85.

_____. "The Roots of Corruption—The Ghanaian Enquiry." *Journal of Modern African Studies* 10, no. 2 (1972):247-66.

Wertheim, F. W. "Sociological Aspects of Corruption in Southeast Asia." *Sociologica Neederlandica* 1, no. 2 (Autumn 1963):129-52.

Woronoff, Jon. *West African Wager*. Metuchen, N.J.: Scarecrow Press, 1972.

Wraith, Ronald, and Simpkins, Edgar. *Corruption in Developing Countries*. London: Allen and Unwin, 1963.

Wurfel, David. "The Philippines." In Richard Rose and Arnold J. Heidenheimer, eds., "Comparative Studies in Political Finance: A Symposium." *Journal of Politics* 25, no. 4 (November 1963): 757–73.

2. Official Documents and Reports

Ghana. *Annual Estimates 1961–62, Part I*. Accra, 1963.

Ghana. *First and Second Report from the Public Accounts Committee of the National Assembly, with Debates Thereon*. Accra, 1965.

Ghana. *Parliamentary Debates. Official Report(s)*. (1969–71) Accra: Ghana Publishing Corp.

Ghana. *Report by the Auditor-General on the Accounts of Ghana for the Period 1st January, 1965 to 30th June, 1966*. Accra, 1968.

Ghana. *Report by the Auditor General on the Accounts of Ghana: First Report for 1971, Local Authorities and Educational Institutions, 1967–68, 1968–69*. Accra, 1971.
Second Report for 1971, Treasury Accounts, 1967–68, 1968–69. Accra, 1971.
Third Report for 1971, Public Boards and Corporations, 1967–68, 1968–69. Accra, 1971.

Ghana. *Report of the Auditor-General on the Accounts of Ghana for the Financial Year Ended 30th June*. . . . Accra. The reports for 1957–58, 1958–59, 1959–60, and 1960–61 were consulted. Each was published the year following the period covered.

Ghana, *Report and Financial Statements by the Accountant-General and Report Thereon by the Auditor-General for the Year Ended 30th September, 1962*. Accra, 1965. The 1962–63 Report had the same title, and was also published in 1965.

Ghana. *Statement by the Government on the Report of the Commission Appointed by Enquire into the Matters Disclosed at the Trial of Captain Benjamin Awaithey Before a Court-Martial, and the Surrounding Circumstances*. White Paper No. 10/59. Accra, 1959.

Ghana. *Statement by the President Concerning Properties and Business Connections of Ministers and Ministerial Secretaries*. Accra, September 1961.

Ghana, Budget Secretariat. *Financial Statement, 1961–62.* Accra, 1963.

Ghana, Commissions and Committees of Inquiry. *See* Appendix A for complete list and citations.

Ghana, Office of Government Statistics. *Labour Statistics, 1959.* Accra: 1960.

Gold Coast Colony. *Report of the Auditor.* Accra. Reports for 1938–39, 1939–40, 1940–41, 1941–42, 1942–43, 1944–45, 1945–46, 1946–47 were consulted. Each was published the year following the fiscal period covered.

Gold Coast. *Report of the Auditor-General on the Accounts of the Gold Coast for the Financial Period ended June 30th . . .* Accra. The Reports for 1955–56 and 1956–57 were consulted. Each was published the year following the financial period covered.

Gold Coast Colony. *Report of the Director of Audit for the Financial Year Ended 31st March . . .* Accra. The Reports for 1947–48, 1948–49, and 1949–50 were consulted. Each was published the year following the fiscal period covered.

Gold Coast. *Report of the Director of Audit on the Accounts of the Gold Coast for the Financial Year Ending 31st March . . .* Accra. The Reports for 1950–51, 1951–52, 1952–53, 1953–54, 1954–55 were consulted. Each was published the year following the fiscal period covered.

India. *Report of the Committee on the Prevention of Corruption.* New Delhi: Ministry of Home Affairs, 1964. [Santhanam Report]

Watson, Aiken (Chairman). *Report of the Commission to Inquire into Disturbances in the Gold Coast.* London: HMSO, 1948, [Watson Commission Report]

3. Newspapers and Other Periodicals

Africa (London)
Afrique Nouvelle (Dakar)
Jeune Afrique (Paris)
New York Times
The Daily Graphic (Accra)

The Ghanaian Times (Accra)
The Legon Observer (Legon)
The Pioneer (Kumasi)
Political Africa (Accra)
The Spokesman (Accra)
The Star (Accra)
The Voice of the People (Accra)
West Africa (London)

Index